WARRIORS & WEAPONS

DUNGEONS & DRAGONS®

WARRIORS & WEAPONS

A Young Adventurer's Guide

WRITTEN BY JIM ZUB

WITH STACY KING AND ANDREW WHEELER

TEN SPEED PRESS
California | New York

CONTENTS

INTRODUCTION

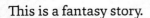

This is a fantasy story.

You are the main character.

Who are you?

What do you do?

This book is a way to answer those two very important questions. It's a guide to the fascinating races that populate the world of DUNGEONS & DRAGONS and the combat-centered classes that define their role as adventurers. It gives you a wide range of options to choose from, along with armor, weapons, and other equipment to outfit your heroic persona.

Read this book from start to finish, or open it to any spot, get pulled in by the exciting illustrations, and start brainstorming from there. The more you read, the more character ideas will spring from your imagination.

Every character is unique. Even when two of them share the same race and class, the decisions they make will take them on an exclusive journey that is yours to tell. DUNGEONS & DRAGONS is all about building memorable characters, and the legends of your grand deeds are about to begin.

Have fun!

HUMAN

DWARF

ELF

GNOME

HALF-ELF

HALF-ORC

HALFLING

DRAGONBORN

KENKU

TABAXI

TIEFLING

TORTLE

FANTASY RACES

Creating a new character involves understanding the traits they share with you and the traits they don't. Part of that comes from inside, their attitudes and personalities, but other parts are outward and physical because in this wondrous world of fantasy, you can be something other than human. By choosing a character's race, you gain a unique appearance and interesting abilities. Each of the twelve options presented here are filled with potential that you can unlock when you decide to make one of them yours and start to build your character's story.

HUMAN

DO YOU LONG TO MAKE YOUR MARK ON THE WORLD?

DO YOU LIVE IN THE MOMENT YET PLAN FOR THE FUTURE?

ARE YOU BRAVE AND AMBITIOUS?

YOU, YES YOU, MIGHT BE A **HUMAN!**

AGE Humans reach adulthood after about two decades and generally live less than a century.

SIZE Adult humans vary wildly in height and build, but most stand between five feet and just over six feet tall and weigh between 100 and 250 pounds.

Humans are the youngest of the common races, late to appear in the world and short-lived compared to dwarves (see page 6), elves (see page 8), and halflings (see page 16). Ambitious and far-reaching, humans make the most of their short lives, whether by exploration, innovation, or the founding of great empires. They are the most adaptable of all the races, and can be found in the remote corners of the world, from vast deserts and tropical islands to mighty mountains and snow-swept plains.

Diversity is a hallmark of the human species. There is no typical appearance—they may be pale to dark skinned, tall or short, with hair that crosses the spectrum of both shade and texture. Their customs, morals, and tastes vary, too. Where they settle, they stay— building cities and kingdoms that persist long after their mortal lifespans have ended. Unlike other races, human communities tend to be welcoming of outsiders as mingling places for all.

Humans who seek adventure are the most daring and ambitious members of a daring and ambitious race. Many are driven by the desire for glory, adventuring to amass power, wealth, and fame. Others are inspired by personal causes, such as a desire to protect their home from danger, to seek out hidden knowledge, or to satisfy their curiosity about the world.

VARIETY IS THE SPICE OF LIFE Humans come from the most varied backgrounds of all characters, giving them access to more knowledge, more languages, and more homeland choices than the other fantasy races.

ATTRIBUTES

Adaptable Humans' flexible nature means that they can easily learn new skills and abilities, giving them an edge when studying or training.

DWARF

DO YOU VALUE HARD WORK AND FAMILY?

DO YOU SOMETIMES HOLD A GRUDGE?

ARE YOU ALWAYS ON THE LOOKOUT FOR TREASURE?

YOU MIGHT BE A DWARF!

AGE Dwarves are recognized as adults by age twenty, but are still considered "young" until age fifty. They live to an average age of 350 years.

SIZE Adult dwarves stand four to five feet tall and weigh around 150 pounds.

Stout and endlessly loyal, dwarves are a people who value tradition and the bonds of clan and family. They are short but strong as well as resilient due to a harsh life on the mountains, making them quite adept for their demanding work as miners.

Dwarven culture is built around mining. Its rewards inform why dwarves have such a powerful appreciation for the splendor of gold and jewels (and the value of solid iron weapons), and its challenges explain why they form such tight-knit communities that are often hostile to possible rivals, most notably goblins and orcs.

Dwarves can be stubborn and single-minded, which means feuds between rival clans can last for generations. Dwarves that bring their crafting skills to cities far from home will never forget where they come from. In fact, honoring a clan tradition or avenging an ancient wrong are common reasons for dwarves to head out on adventures, though they might also go exploring for the sake of personal glory, in service to one of their industrious gods, or simply for the chance to get more gold!

DWARVEN FEUDS
Dwarves have a strong sense of justice and deep loyalty to their clan traditions. A wrong done to one dwarf is considered a slight against the entire clan, which means one insult, if not apologized for quickly enough, can become a full-blown clan feud lasting for generations.

ATTRIBUTES

Tough Physically robust, dwarves can take a lot of hits, and they have a natural resistance to poison.

Handy Dwarves love to develop their expertise in certain crafts, whether it's forging weapons or cutting stone. They know the tools of their trade inside out.

Strong Dwarves that live in tough terrain, like cold and rugged mountains, are particularly noted for their physical strength.

Wise Dwarves that live in less hostile terrain tend to be highly perceptive. Away from the shelter of their mines, they've learned to keep their wits about them.

ELF

DO YOU LOVE MAGIC AND ARCANE MYSTERIES?

DO YOU FEEL OLDER AND WISER THAN YOUR YEARS?

DO YOU PREFER DIPLOMACY RATHER THAN PHYSICAL CONFRONTATION?

YOU MIGHT BE An **ELF**!

SIZE Elves are generally a bit shorter than humans. They are typically very slender and beautiful!

AGE Elves mature at about the same rate as humans but consider themselves childlike and inexperienced until about their 100th birthday. They typically live for more than 700 years.

There are places in the world that don't quite seem real; areas of breathtaking beauty where the magic of other realms spills through into our own. It's in these locations that you're most likely to encounter elves, a race known for their elegance, grace, and gifts of enchantment.

Born of otherworldly magic, elves live for centuries, and often seem unfazed by the presence and actions of more short-lived creatures. They prefer to remain in their own secluded communities, but may venture out to share their artistic gifts or martial skills with the world, or to expand their understanding of other cultures. Elves cherish diplomacy and avoid violence if they can, preferring to rely on civility and cunning to resolve conflicts. An elf might master swordplay without ever engaging in actual battle!

Elven society generally falls into three categories. High elves are the most refined, the most haughty, and the most devoted to magic. Wood elves are in touch with the natural world and the skills needed to survive in the wild. Dark elves, also called drow, have adapted to life underground. Though they have a reputation for wickedness, one must never be too quick to judge. After all, being predictable is boring, and elves hate to be boring.

FAVORED WEAPONS Elves excel at armed combat and specialize in different weapons, such as longswords, longbows, crossbows, and rapiers.

ATTRIBUTES

Grace Elves are as dexterous in combat as they are in dance.

Magic Naturally gifted in magic, many elves can perform some simple spells without any study, and all elves have a high resistance to enchantment.

Vigilance Elves have refined senses. They can see clearly in the dark and are very alert to strange sights and sounds. Elves do not need sleep, which makes them excellent at performing watch duties!

GNOME

ARE YOU FASCINATED BY HOW THE WORLD WORKS?

DO YOU SOMETIMES TALK TOO MUCH?

DO YOU LONG TO SEE THE WORLD AND MAKE NEW FRIENDS ALONG THE WAY?

YOU MIGHT BE A GNOME!

SIZE Adult gnomes stand just over three feet tall, about half the height of a tall human. They weigh about 45 pounds.

AGE Gnomes reach adulthood by about age twenty and live for 350 to 500 years.

The small bodies of gnomes hold big personalities, filled with humor, happiness, and positivity that shine forth from their smiling faces. They live in bustling communities carved out of hillsides, where the sounds of hard work and laughter fill the air, though many of them will travel far and wide to seek out adventure and get as much excitement out of life as they can. They always see the best in other people and will often be enthusiastic to join an adventuring party, though their talkativeness can be exhausting for some. They have a lot to say and are happy to share it all!

Gnomes' love of learning makes itself known in their passion for taking on hobbies—and because they live long lives, they can hone their skills in fine crafts, such as woodworking, engineering, inventing, or the study of magic and alchemy. Gnomes never worry about making mistakes, because every error is another opportunity to learn and grow. If there is a bright side to any situation, or a positive way to look at any encounter, a gnome will find it.

GNOMISH NAMES
Gnomes love names, and most have a half-dozen or so! These range from the formal, three-part names they use around non-gnomes to affectionate nicknames bestowed by family and friends. Gnomes favor names that are fun to say, such as Zook, Boddynock, Ellyjobell, or Stumbleduck.

ATTRIBUTES

Intellect Gnomes are known for their wit, charm, and smarts, and will often try to talk their way out of difficult situations.

Industrious Many gnomes are natural tinkerers who build wonderful clockwork toys and devices.

Dexterity Gnomes have strong reflexes and an excellent sense of balance. They might prefer to duck out of a fight rather than fight back.

Tricky Many gnomes have a gift for stealth and illusion, allowing them to mask their presence or easily slip away from trouble.

HALF-ELF

ARE YOU SOMETIMES IMPULSIVE AND PRONE TO WANDERING?

DO YOU FEEL TRAPPED BETWEEN TWO DIFFERENT WORLDS?

DO YOU VALUE PERSONAL EXPRESSION AND FREEDOM ABOVE SOCIAL TIES?

YOU MIGHT BE A **HALF-ELF!**

HALF-ELF NAMES Half-elves raised among humans are often given elvish names, and vice versa.

AGE Half-elves mature much like humans, reaching adulthood in their early twenties, but live much longer—often more than 180 years!

SIZE Half-elves are about the same size as humans, ranging from five to six feet tall and weighing between 100 and 180 pounds.

Born between two worlds but belonging to neither, half-elves are conceived in rare romances between mortal humans and mystic elves. As such, they combine the best qualities of both: human curiosity and ambition softened by the refined senses and artistry of the elves.

Half-elves are also destined to live apart from society. Among elves, they become grown adults while their peers remain children; among humans, they watch friends and family age while they themselves carry on seemingly untouched by time. Many choose solitary lives as a result, although others take advantage of their natural charm and grace to find a place at the heart of their communities, serving as leaders and diplomats. Their long lives often lead to wandering, drawing them into an adventurer's existence among other misfits who understand their outsider status.

Half-elves appear elvish to humans and human to elves. Their features may be a perfect blend of both parents, or favor one side of their heritage over the other. Their eyes are usually elven, large and luminous in shades of gold or silver. Half-elf men may grow facial hair, and some adopt a beard to conceal their elven lineage. Their chaotic spirits value personal freedom above all, and they fare poorly when bound by too many rules or expectations.

ATTRIBUTES

Darkvision Elven heritage has gifted half-elves with superior vision in dark and low-light conditions.

Fey Ancestry The magic of their fairy ancestors makes half-elves immune to sleep spells. They are also difficult to charm by magical means.

Charisma Half-elves combine the grace of elves with the appeal of humans, making it easy for them to find friends wherever they go!

Chaotic Spirit Like their elven forebears, half-elves are drawn to chaos. They find creative solutions to problems but can be unpredictable at times!

HALF-ORC

DO YOU HAVE STRONG
EMOTIONS—BOTH JOY
AND RAGE?

ARE YOU DETERMINED
AND STUBBORN?

DO YOU VALUE ACTION
OVER CONTEMPLATION?

YOU MIGHT BE A HALF-ORC!

AGE Half-orcs mature faster than humans and are considered adults after 14 years. They continue to age more rapidly throughout their lives, rarely surviving more than 75 years.

SCARS Among orcs, scars are an important mark of status. Battle scars denote victory, while other wounds serve as badges of shame or punishment. Any half-orc who has lived among orcs will bear such scars, whether good or bad. Some hide these marks when among non-orcs, while others flaunt their scars to intimidate enemies or honor their heritage.

SIZE Half-orcs are larger and bulkier than humans. They range from six to seven feet tall and weigh between 180 and 250 pounds.

Where human and orc communities have learned to live in harmony, half-orcs may be found. Even when raised by humans, there is no hiding their heritage: their grayish skin, sloping foreheads, prominent teeth, and towering builds make it clear that they have orcish blood. Half-orcs most often live within orc communities, although some may be raised within human settlements.

The rage felt by all orcs runs through half-orc veins, burning like fire. Half-orcs feel all their emotions deeply, whether blinding fury or boisterous glee. Insults deeply strike their pride, and sadness saps their strength. Physical pleasures—such as feasting, wrestling, and wild dancing—bring them great joy. They are often short-tempered and sullen, and it takes little for an argument to escalate into a fight.

Half-orcs struggle to find acceptance wherever they go. Many races, including humans, distrust them, while fellow orcs may taunt or bully them because of their perceived diminutive size. While some half-orcs are content to survive solely on brute strength, others are driven to prove their worth to the wider world. With their physical prowess and relentless nature, half-orcs make fearsome adventurers, renowned for their mighty deeds and notorious for their savage fury.

ATTRIBUTES

Relentless Endurance When badly injured, half-orcs can call upon great reserves of strength and energy to avoid unconsciousness, staying on their feet to continue the battle.

Savage Attacks When they make a critical hit, half-orcs can add their innate brute strength to the blow, increasing the damage significantly.

Menace Their size and rough appearance makes it easy for half-orcs to intimidate others! They can often bluff their way out of a fight—although most prefer to let their fists swing.

Darkvision Their orcish heritage gives half-orcs superior vision in dark and low-light conditions.

HALFLING

DO YOU SEE THE GOOD IN EVERYONE?

DO YOU VALUE FAMILY AND FRIENDS OVER FAME AND FORTUNE?

ARE YOU BRAVE ENOUGH TO FACE DANGERS MANY TIMES YOUR SIZE?

YOU MIGHT BE A **HALFLING!**

SIZE Adult halflings stand about three feet tall and weigh 40 to 45 pounds.

AGE Halflings are considered adults by age twenty and can live up to 150 years.

Halflings are friendly, cheerful people inspired by the values of family, home, and simple pleasures. Short and stout, they like to wear bright colors that contrast with their ruddy skin, brown to hazel eyes, and brown hair. Most live in small, peaceful communities within the kingdoms of other races. Displays of wealth and status don't impress them, and there is no halfling royalty. Instead they are ruled by the wisdom of their elders, although there is always room for capable young halflings to make a name for themselves.

Halflings are a curious people, interested in even the most ordinary details about the world. This curiosity, rather than a love of gold or glory, is the inspiration for most young halflings who become adventurers. Others are driven by a danger to their community, putting themselves at risk to protect their families and their friends. Halflings excel at finding simple, practical solutions to problems and bring a touch of home comforts wherever they go. Many an adventuring party has been grateful for the warmth and good cheer that a halfling companion can create in even the most desolate of dungeons!

THE UNSEEN HALFLING

Their small size and innate stealth help halflings excel at avoiding unwanted attention. They can slip through busy crowds without being noticed, giving them a great advantage when gathering information or sneaking away from a fight!

ATTRIBUTES

Luck Their knack for finding practical solutions can sometimes give halflings a second chance to correct their mistakes.

Bravery Stout of heart as well as of body, halflings will face dangers that cause other adventurers to flee.

Nimbleness Because they are so small, halflings can evade the attacks of larger creatures!

Stealth Their short stature makes it easy for halflings to hide and avoid unwanted attention.

DRAGONBORN

AGE Dragonborn mature quickly, reaching full adulthood by the age of 15 years. They live to around 80 years old. Dragonborn commonly have one simple name in childhood and take on a different moniker to mark their transition into adulthood.

DRAGONBORN COLORS Most dragonborn scales are brass or bronze in tone. Red, rust, copper-green, and gold hues are also common. A few clans still have a strong bloodline connection to their founding dragon and, in these rare cases, brighter colors, including blue, green, and shining white, can be found.

SIZE Dragonborn are usually taller than most humans, and much more heavily built, with thick hides that make them heavier still. They lack the wings and tails of their dragon relatives, however.

Dragons are some of the most powerful and terrifying creatures you might ever meet. Their humanoid kin, the dragonborn, are a lot more approachable, but still kind of scary!

Descended from dragons and shaped by draconic magic, dragonborn are a noble warrior race, with dragonlike features and powers inherited from their ancestors. These skills are tied to specific types of destructive energy, which are often reflected in the color of the dragonborn's scaly hide. They live in clans that are often linked to a specific class of dragon ancestor, and they proudly worship their dragon gods. Clans are the heart of dragonborn society, and all dragonborn know their duty and strive to serve to their best abilities, whether that means being a great warrior, a great craftsperson, or a great cook. Failure brings shame to the clan, and excellence brings honor. As descendants of arguably the most noble and mighty of all creatures, they feel they have a lot to live up to.

Dragonborn will rarely look beyond their clans for assistance, yet they find that sometimes the best way to serve their clan and honor their gods is to leave everything behind and set out on an adventure, pursuing a great quest or bringing glory to their people.

ATTRIBUTES

Strength Draconic heritage imbues all dragonborn with great physical power.

Breath Weapon Dragonborn can exhale the type of destructive energy associated with their ancestry! Some dragonborn breathe fire, but others expel bolts of lightning, bursts of cold, streams of acid, or clouds of poison.

Resistance Dragonborn have a natural resistance to whatever destructive energy they possess, so a dragonborn who breathes fire is immune to fire, and a dragonborn who breathes acid is invulnerable to acid.

KENKU

AGE A short-lived species, kenku reach maturity at 12 years old and can live up to 60 years.

AN ANCIENT CURSE The kenku once served a powerful entity on another plane of existence. When their master learned of a kenku plot to steal a beautiful treasure, the entity imposed three dreadful punishments upon them.

- Their beloved wings were stripped away.
- Their creative spark was snuffed out.
- Their voices were stolen.

SIZE Kenku are smaller than humans, around five feet tall. They weigh between 90 and 120 pounds.

Haunted by an ancient crime that cursed their species, kenku wander the world as vagabonds and thieves. Stripped of their wings as retribution, all kenku are driven by the desire to fly once more. Many take up spellcasting in the hopes of achieving this dream, while others search the world for magical items rumored to give the gift of flight. They are drawn to the sky, flitting around tall towers or high on mountaintops. Unable to settle for long, they live temporarily on the fringes of other creatures' communities before their wandering spirit moves them along to the next patch of lost sky.

The curse has stolen the kenkus' creative spark. They can speak only in sounds that they have heard before, and they write, draw, or otherwise create only what they have already seen. Their individual names come from the sounds they can reproduce, while non-kenku use a description of this sound in place of a name. They have a talent for learning and memorizing details, making them excellent scouts and spies, and many earn their living by plagiarism and theft.

The most ambitious and daring of kenku may strike out on their own as adventurers. They dislike solitude and will partner eagerly with fellow heroes, mimicking the voices and words of their companions. Kenku are able to replicate humanoid languages along with sounds, and they often combine overheard phrases with natural noises to convey their meaning.

ATTRIBUTES

Expert Forgers Kenku have a mystical ability to duplicate the handwriting and craftwork of other creatures, making them excellent forgers.

Mimicry Kenku can impersonate sounds with eerie accuracy, including voices. Another creature would need to listen very carefully in order to detect that it's fake!

TABAXI

FELINE FIXATIONS All tabaxi have quirks that reflect their catlike natures. Some purr when pleased, others lash their tails angrily when upset. Some can't resist napping in a patch of sunlight, while others constantly fidget with a ball of yarn in their pocket.

SIZE Tabaxi are generally a little taller than humans, with the slender bodies and long winding tails of cats!

AGE Tabaxi age at the same rate as humans.

Somewhere beyond the charted world is a distant, sunbaked land of catlike people called the tabaxi. A rare few have wandered outside their borders in search of stories, secrets, and lore. Their curiosity is boundless but their interests can be fickle. One day they may feel driven to study the legend of a famous warlock, and the next they may seek buried pirate treasure. The world is a puzzle box full of surprises, and tabaxi want to uncover them all.

Naturally agile and charismatic, tabaxi make excellent performers, often traveling in troupes as actors, acrobats, jugglers, and minstrels. This arrangement allows them to constantly visit new places and meet new people, never settling anywhere for long. Of course, joining an adventuring party also gives opportunities for excitement and discovery.

Tabaxi believe they are the creation of a trickster god named the Cat Lord, who imbues them with their catlike qualities and watches over them on their travels.

ATTRIBUTES

Claws Tabaxi can deliver a dangerous strike from their hands or feet, or clamber up walls and other surfaces with ease.

Nimbleness Tabaxi usually land on their feet, and can move extra fast when circumstances demand it— useful for making a quick getaway.

Stealth Tabaxi have a knack for slinking into shadows and observing from the darkness.

Perception Tabaxi can see in the dark and are unusually alert to the presence of others.

TIEFLING

TIEFLING NAMES Some tieflings are given names that reflect their infernal heritage and bring to mind dark magics. Others are named after a virtue or ideal, hoping they will live up to the values embodied by their moniker.

AGE Tieflings age at the same rate as humans and live a little longer.

SIZE Tieflings are similar in size than humans, although their horns and imposing auras may make them seem taller than they are!

DO YOU SOMETIMES FEEL LIKE YOU DON'T FIT IN?

ARE YOU USED TO RELYING ONLY ON YOURSELF TO GET THINGS DONE?

DO YOU TRUST THOSE CLOSE TO YOU, BUT KEEP OTHERS AT ARM'S LENGTH?

YOU MIGHT BE A TIEFLING!

Tieflings are not a true race, as they are not connected by a common bloodline. Instead, they are beings born to ordinary humans who have been touched by the darkest of magics.

With their long tails, horns, sharp teeth, and strange pupil-less eyes, tieflings are cursed to resemble devils. Some are defiantly proud of their appearance, decorating their horns or tails with jewels or precious metals, while others try to disguise these features. Their diabolical traits include a natural talent for magic.

Tieflings face considerable prejudice. They are often rejected by their communities, or even their families, so they head out into the world on their own, mistrusted by everyone they encounter. In turn, they tend to be distrustful of others as well.

Despite what superstitious strangers may think of them, tieflings are not inclined toward evil. Their cursed bloodlines determine their appearance, not their character. Yet, because of how they look, they are often denied work, lodging, or a fair chance to prove themselves. The life of an adventurer offers one path for tieflings determined to prove their virtue.

ATTRIBUTES

Presence Tieflings are noted for their magnetic charm. Even people who don't like or trust them will usually find them fascinating.

Fire Resistance Their infernal blood gives tieflings a natural resistance to fire and heat.

Hellfire Attacking a tiefling can be a dangerous gamble, as they can sometimes strike back instantly, consuming their attacker in flames!

Darkness Tieflings have the innate magical ability to create a cloud of shadow that's impenetrable, even to those with darkvision!

TORTLE

ARE YOU FRIENDLY AND
EASY TO GET ALONG WITH?

ARE YOU FASCINATED BY
THE BEAUTY AND VARIETY
OF NATURE?

DO YOU LOVE THE COMFORTS
OF HOME, BUT STILL WONDER
WHAT LIES BEYOND THE
HORIZON?

YOU MIGHT BE A **TORTLE!**

AGE Tortles live for about 50 years. Their infancy lasts less than a year, and they reach adulthood by age fifteen. Tortles take a mate only in the final years of their lives, and spend that time raising their offspring in special fortified hatcheries, preparing the young for their lives ahead.

SIZE Adult tortles grow up to six feet tall, but they are much stockier and heavier than humans of similar height, because of both their thickset build and their dense armored shells, which account for about a third of their weight.

26

For tortles, life begins and ends on the beach—and the time in between is often spent there as well! This semiaquatic reptilian race of humanoids begins their lives hatched from eggs on a beach, and ends their lives protecting the eggs of the next generation. The tortoise-like shells on their backs are the only homes they will ever need, so they often live out in the wilderness, developing excellent survival skills such as fishing, hunting, and trapping.

Even-tempered and positive, tortles are always happy in their own company. They appreciate nature and solitude but also enjoy the comraderie of others and they love to make new friends.

Despite their general air of contentment, most tortles will experience a wanderlust at some point in their lives and head off to explore the world with nothing but their person. They're keen to see the variety of life and engage other cultures, though they will likely never settle anywhere for long, especially if they're expected to live with a roof above their heads.

UNDER DAY AND NIGHT
Tortles believe that day and night watch over them, with the sun and the moon being the "eyes" of these protective forces. Any time both can be seen in the sky is considered blessed, and tortles are nervous when neither is visible. And they hate being underground!

ATTRIBUTES

Protection Tortles don't wear armor, but their shells offer a robust natural defense, and they can disappear into their shells for extra protection.

Strength Carrying a heavy shell everywhere really helps build the muscles!

Holding Breath Tortles cannot breathe underwater, but they can hold their breath for up to an hour—a useful talent for sea fishing, but also handy when there's poison in the air.

Claws The sharp claws of a tortle, paired with their natural strength, can do some serious damage.

BARBARIAN

FIGHTER

MONK

PALADIN

RANGER

ROGUE

CHARACTER CLASSES

The class you choose for your character is more than a profession—it's a calling! Classes shape not only what they can do, but what kind of person they are, as well as the way your character thinks about the world and interacts with others. For example, a barbarian might see the world as a constant struggle for survival, where brute strength and cunning are all that matter, while a paladin would filter interactions through the lens of faith, always aware of the holy battle between good and evil. A rogue would have contacts among thieves, spies, and other nefarious types, while a ranger would know foresters and innkeepers spread across the wild lands.

Your class provides special features, such as a fighter's mastery of weapons and armor, or a rogue's expertise with stealth. When you first start out, your skills won't be specialized, but as you gain experience, your character will grow and change, unlocking new abilities and powers. Choose your class wisely, for it will shape the hero you become!

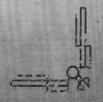

BARBARIAN

ARE YOU FEARLESS IN THE FACE OF DANGER?

DO YOU PREFER NATURE INSTEAD OF BIG CITIES?

DO YOU SOMETIMES LOSE YOURSELF IN ANGER?

YOU MIGHT MAKE A GOOD BARBARIAN!

PRIMAL PATHS Although all barbarians share a rage they call upon in times of need, where that anger comes from and how they feel about it can be quite different. Some barbarians consider their anger a curse, others see it as a blessing. Depending on what their belief entails, a barbarian may prescribe to a certain primal path.

PATH OF THE ANCESTRAL GUARDIAN
Ancestral Guardians communicate with powerful warriors from the past to gain strength from them in combat. Ancestral Guardians are part of a great lineage.

PATH OF THE BERSERKER
Berserkers thrill at combat and let their anger overwhelm them in a joyous display of violence. They're dangerous and effective.

PATH OF THE TOTEM WARRIOR
Totem Warriors accept a spirit animal as a guide, protector, and inspiration. The barbarian's rage is a gift given to them as part of their journey to enlightenment.

Barbarians are warriors of rage. They call upon deep wells of anger from within or draw on the fury of their ancestral spirits to grant them power and strength in their times of need. When your enemies outnumber you and things look lost, a barbarian's fearless combat abilities can turn the tide.

During combat, barbarians will charge into the fray without any hesitation. They know their place is up front, making sure all eyes are on them as they scream a war cry or roar with unmatched fury.

A barbarian's intense emotions guide their actions. Some are very protective of their communities and stay close to home, while others wander far in search of adventure and the thrill of battle.

EQUIPMENT AND ATTRIBUTES

Armor Barbarians wear light or medium armor (see pages 80 and 82). They want to make sure that any armor they do wear won't impede their movement in battle.

Weapons Barbarians tend to have large and loud weapons that work well with their rage-fueled attacks—hammers, battle axes, two-handed swords, and the like. They appreciate weapons that intimidate their foes and make them look even more fearsome than they already are.

Rage Barbarians have a primal ferocity they call upon in times of great stress. This rage helps them focus their attacks and enhance their strength. It also helps them shrug off blows and ignore pain for as long as their fury lasts. A raging barbarian is a scary sight to behold if they're your enemy, but their courage and passion in the heat of battle is also very inspiring to their allies.

Danger Sense Barbarians may seem reckless, but their senses are quite sharp. They're deeply in touch with their emotions and intuition, and it gives them an uncanny sense of when things around them aren't as they should be. When a barbarian perceives something wrong, get ready!

WULFGAR THE WARHAMMER

TEMPERED RAGE Like all barbarians, Wulfgar calls upon his internal anger to aid him in battle and shrug off wounds, but Wulfgar is not the type to relish these moments of rage. The time he spent with Bruenor Battlehammer (see page 36), a dwarven fighter who started as his enemy but over time became like a father to him, taught Wulfgar a lot about self-control and honor in battle.

Wulfgar is a famous human barbarian warrior who grew up in a northern land called Icewind Dale. As a member of the Tribe of the Elk, he learned how to hunt, forage, survive harsh winters, and defend his people from creatures and invading armies.

Facing Wulgar in combat is a terrifying prospect—he stands almost seven feet tall and weighs 350 pounds. His strength is incredible to behold, especially when swinging Aegis-Fang, his magical warhammer. With that mythic weapon at his side, Wulfgar has driven back invaders and defeated dragons. Facing Wulfgar head-on is a recipe for disaster, so only the most agile and careful have a chance of holding their own against him.

PLAYING WULFGAR

Wulfgar is not subtle or careful. He's direct, focused, confident, and always ready for combat. Growing up in a barbarian tribe has left him without much knowledge of cities, especially those in the south, and he feels ill at ease around too many people. Wulfgar thrives in cold open air and it is where he feels most at home.

AEGIS-FANG

Aegis-Fang is a legendary weapon for a legendary warrior. Forged by Bruenor Battlehammer and imbued with powerful dwarven magic, the head of the hammer is made from pure mithral with a diamond coating magically adhered during the forging process and an adamantine shaft. Its head is engraved with the magical inscriptions of Clangeddin, the dwarven god of battle, as well as the symbols of Moradin, the dwarven god of creation, and Dumathoin, keeper of secrets under the mountain.

Most people would have difficulty even lifting Aegis-Fang, but Wulfgar is well trained with the weapon and able to swing it with ease. Even more amazing, it will magically return to Wulfgar's hand at his command, allowing him to throw it at enemies and then get right it back, pummeling those who dare to stand in his way.

FIGHTER

DO YOU LIKE THE IDEA OF CHARGING INTO BATTLE?

ARE YOU UP FRONT AND READY FOR ACTION?

CAN YOU KEEP A COOL HEAD WHEN THINGS GET INTENSE?

YOU MIGHT MAKE A GOOD FIGHTER!

MARTIAL ARCHETYPES

With so many different fighters out there, having a focal point for your skills can be valuable. There are many archetypes, but here a few examples to help inspire you.

BATTLE MASTER

These fighters carry on enduring traditions of combat and weapon mastery passed down through generations. Studying the techniques of the past gives them knowledge they bring to future conflicts.

CHAMPION

These fighters focus on raw power and strength, honing their physical prowess to deadly perfection.

ELDRITCH KNIGHT

These fighters supplement their battle skills with a bit of magic knowledge, wielding spells that can enhance their abilities and surprise their enemies.

Soldiers, warriors, gladiators, mercenaries, bodyguards—there are as many different types of fighters as there are conflicts needing to be fought with weapon in hand. What all of these occupations share is a mastery of melee combat and a desire to stare down death and not give up.

Fighters encompass a wide range of combatants. There are those who use size and strength to gain the upper hand in battle, yet a number are dexterous or stealthy. Some are adept at long-range fighting with bows or spears, while others wade into hand-to-hand combat with a sword and shield, a polearm, or any other weapon in which they're trained. Whatever their methods or equipment, fighters are almost always at the front line of combat, charging forward to engage their enemies and protect their friends from harm.

EQUIPMENT AND ATTRIBUTES

Armor Fighters are trained to wear any type of armor, from light cloth or hide all the way up to full plate with a shield. Whatever is required, a fighter can wear it.

Weapons Fighters are trained with all regular and martial weaponry, giving them a deep pool from which to choose. Many also have specialized training with unusual weapons, so feel free to get creative.

Second Wind After long days of adventure and combat, when most other adventurers would be exhausted and lose momentum, fighters can dig deep within themselves to regain their strength and keep going. Their resolve inspires the rest of their group to push past adversity.

BRUENOR BATTLEHAMMER

MASTER BLACKSMITH More than just a warrior, Bruenor is also a brilliant smithy, able to forge powerful dwarven weapons from even the most difficult materials. The art of crafting a weapon from raw materials and building each component to its proper strength and balance is his lifelong pursuit. Bruenor trained for many years to understand how weapons are made, and it gives him a greater appreciation for how they're used in combat.

Bruenor Battlehammer is a famous dwarven fighter known for his gruff demeanor and impressive fighting skills. Loyal to his friends and vicious to his enemies, Bruenor longed for the day when he and his people could reclaim their ancestral home, the dwarven fortress known as Mithral Hall, from the evil shadow dragon known as Shimmergloom. In time, Bruenor would find a way to make that dream a reality, and it would lead him to be crowned King of Mithral Hall.

In his prime, Bruenor was known for wearing a one-horned helmet, wielding a single-bladed axe, and carrying a shield emblazoned with a foaming mug sigil (the symbol of Clan Battlehammer).

PLAYING BRUENOR

Bruenor is abrupt and stubborn, even more so than regular dwarves, who are already known for their dour attitude. In conversation, he doesn't waste time, and that direct approach carries through all his interactions, social and physical.

A headstrong curmudgeon, Bruenor is hard on his friends and family, expecting them to do their best no matter what situation they find themselves in. He's just as hard on himself, pushing his physical limits and charging first into battle so others don't get hurt. Bruenor is a true hero, courageous and caring, even if he doesn't let it show on the surface.

FLAMETONGUE

Bruenor's magic axe, Flametongue, bursts into flame upon his command, creating light and burning foes even as its blade cuts deep. Bruenor becomes the center of attention in combat when he fearlessly raises Flametongue as magical fire pours forth; allies rally around as they rush into battle. A dwarven army at Bruenor's command is an awe-inspiring sight on the battlefield.

MONK

DO YOU WANT TO HARNESS THE MYSTICAL POWER THAT LIES WITHIN?

ARE YOU NIMBLE YET STRONG?

CAN YOU HANDLE THE RIGORS OF A MONASTIC LIFE?

YOU MIGHT MAKE A GOOD MONK!

MONASTERY LIFE Monasteries are typically small, walled communities where monks live a simple, structured life focused on training, study, and, sometimes, farming. While some compounds are isolated, others interact freely with their neighbors, trading their services for food and goods.

Many monks enter the monastery as children, sent to live there because they had been orphaned or their parents could no longer feed them. Others are sent by their parents in gratitude for some service the monks had performed to help their family.

Monks dedicate their lives to the study of a mystical force called ki, which flows through all living creatures in the world. They learn to harness this energy within their own bodies, channeling it into powerful blows and elegant dodges that display uncanny speed and strength. These graceful fighters shun complex weapons and armor, relying upon the power that lies within to achieve their victories!

The life of a monk begins in childhood, when they live in tight-knit communities and their daily training follows a rigid routine. Becoming an adventurer means leaving this structure behind, a harsh transition that few undertake lightly. Adventuring monks generally do not value gold or glory, focusing instead on the pursuit of self-improvement and spiritual enlightenment.

EQUIPMENT AND ATTRIBUTES

Armor Monks choose not to wear any type of armor, since it interferes with the flow of ki.

Weapons Monks can use simple weapons and short swords. They favor inexpensive weapons such as staffs and clubs that can move with the flow of their martial attacks.

Ki A monk's training allows them to harness the mystical power of ki. This energy allows them to make extra unarmed blows after an attack, improve their ability to dodge, or even disengage from battle with a powerful jump. In the beginning, access to ki is limited, but as monks become more skilled, the amount of ki they harness also grows. Experienced monks are capable of astonishing, supernatural feats using their ki!

Martial Training Most monks begin training in the martial arts at a young age. They may have studied broadly, gaining a basic competence in a wide range of fighting styles, or chosen to focus their training on a single skill, mastering a specific weapon or unarmed attack. Their training emphasizes a flowing, dexterous approach to combat; witnessing a monk in battle is like watching a complex, elegant dance.

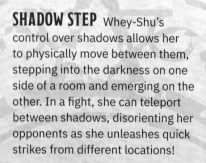

LEGENDARY MONK

WHEY-SHU

SHADOW STEP Whey-Shu's control over shadows allows her to physically move between them, stepping into the darkness on one side of a room and emerging on the other. In a fight, she can teleport between shadows, disorienting her opponents as she unleashes quick strikes from different locations!

CLOAK OF SHADOW Through the power of her ki, Whey-Shu can become one with the darkness. Unless in a very brightly lit space, she can magically wrap shadows around her body, concealing her from view. In combat, she uses this ability to devastating effect, striking unseen and then vanishing again before her opponent can land a single blow!

PLAYING WHEY-SHU Whey-Shu is quiet but confident, willing to let others talk while she observes and plans. Once she decides to act, she is swift and determined. Her goal is to end a conflict as quickly as possible. If she miscalculates her enemy's strength, she will retreat and reassess before trying again. What matters most to her is the result, not individual setbacks along the way.

There is a famous kenku monk known as Whey-Shu, but that's not her actual name. It's just the closest sound most humanoids can make to her true name, the sound of a soft slipper sliding across a wooden floor. Whey-Shu's name reflects both her monastic training and her quiet presence, behind which she conceals considerable power.

After her kenku flock was saved from a goblin invasion by dwarven monks, Whey-Shu's parents gave her, their youngest child, to the monastery in gratitude. Her inability to communicate relegated her to the role of a lowly servant, and she was assigned to cleaning duties and making copies of sacred texts. Her kenku gift for mimicry soon led her to spend nights practicing the techniques from the scrolls she spent the day transcribing. By the time the monks discovered Whey-Shu's secret training regiment, she had developed incredible control over ki power that rivaled many adults. Despite her youth, Whey-Shu is now widely regarded as one of the masters of the Way of the Shadow, a monastic tradition that emphasizes stealth and subterfuge.

THE WAY OF THE SHADOW

One monastic tradition focuses on the use of ki energy to manipulate shadows and darkness—the Way of the Shadow. Known as shadowdancers, such monks often serve as spies and assassins. Like mercenaries, they are hired by any who can afford their fees. Whey-Shu doesn't mind working for others for money. The one exception is fighting goblins—she still has vivid memories of the invasion that endangered her family and eagerly battles goblins free of charge.

PALADIN

DO YOU LONG TO SERVE A NOBLE CAUSE?

ARE YOU EQUALLY HAPPY HELPING FRIENDS AND SMITING ENEMIES?

DO YOU WANT TO BE THE BEST AT BEING GOOD?

YOU MIGHT BE A PALADIN!

SACRED OATHS Paladins use magic with power derived from a commitment to their gods. To that end, all paladins must swear a holy oath that grants them special spells and abilities. If paladins fail to live up to their pledge, they may be cut off from these powers.

OATH OF THE ANCIENTS
Paladins who take this oath are dedicated to love and kindness. They have the power to channel the wrath of nature and use other nature-based spells.

OATH OF DEVOTION
Paladins who take this oath are dedicated to the causes of honesty, virtue, and compassion. They can bless their weapons and use spells of protection and revelation.

OATH OF VENGEANCE
Paladins who take this oath are dedicated to punishment and retribution. They can grant themselves advantage in battle and use other spells to help destroy their enemies.

Some adventurers seek glory, some seek wealth, and some seek excitement, but paladins pursue a life of adventure in service to a higher calling. They are warriors and champions of righteousness who fight the wicked and save the innocent because they've been called by their god or gods to do so. And their gods imbue them with divine gifts to make them better servants. However, if a paladin ever fails to live up to their gods' ideals, they may find their divine powers leaving them.

Paladins are skilled warriors with expertise in many weapons and fighting styles, but they're also adept spellcasters who channel the power of their gods to help or heal those around them, or to smite their foes with a single devastating blow. Paladins are typically very disciplined fighters who head into battle with clear purpose and unshakeable principles.

EQUIPMENT AND ATTRIBUTES

Armor Like fighters, paladins are trained to wear any type of armor, from light cloth or hide all the way up to full plate with a shield.

Weapons Paladins are trained with all regular and martial weaponry, so they have many options when heading into battle.

Healing Touch Paladins are blessed with the ability to heal wounds, cure disease, or remove poisons by laying on hands. Paladins are immune to disease because of the power flowing through them.

Divine Powers Devotion to their gods gives paladins special abilities, including the power to sense whether a person is wicked or good and the power to channel divine energy into a strike known as Divine Smite. Some paladins can also project an aura that protects or inspires those around them.

Martial Prowess Paladins are soldiers of faith, and they are well trained in the ways of battle. Some choose to be great defensive fighters, protecting those in trouble. Others choose to be great offensive fighters, putting all their energy into smiting!

LEGENDARY PALADIN REDCLAY

CLEANSING FIRE As a dragonborn with fire dragon ancestry, Redclay was born with the ability to breathe fire, but as a master paladin she has a much more devastating ability. For brief periods of time, Redclay can surround herself, and her allies, with a wall of divine flame that destroys nearby enemies while leaving those enclosed untouched by the blaze.

PRAYER OF HEALING Redclay is a devotee of Bahamut, the draconic god of justice. Through her prayers to him, Redclay can heal the sick and injured. She offers particular care to those afflicted by madness or delusion, believing the mad should be restored, not punished.

44

An orphan dragonborn raised in a remote mountain monastery dedicated to the draconic god Bahamut, Redclay first came to notice one brutal winter when her home was besieged by an army of orcs seeking control of the mountains. A month into the siege, with food almost all gone, Redclay slipped out of the monastery and passed through the enemy camp undetected. She returned leading an army of Bahamut faithful and headed a cavalry charge that broke the siege apart. She was 13 years old.

After becoming a celebrated figure, Redclay was named a general of her clan. Yet she found that neither the life of a soldier nor the life of a monk quite suited her, so she became a paladin, seeking out those most in need of aid and giving them hope when all seemed lost.

Though still quite small for a dragonborn, and so youthful that she retains her childhood name, Redclay is widely respected for the strength of her faith and the scale of her accomplishments.

PLAYING REDCLAY

Redclay is a devout and humble warrior who lives a simple life of service to others. Her chosen cause is to help people of good character who are suffering from injustice and have nowhere else to turn. Though she is content to pursue her crusade alone, she will gladly accept the aid of traveling companions if they are also above repute. She will always put the needs of others ahead of her own.

THE WAR DRUM OF BAHAMUT

Redclay's fame makes her an inspiring figure, but she also possesses a drum, given to her by the monks, that can magically inspire all those who fight at her side. Any ally of Redclay within earshot when she plays the drum before battle receives a boost to their courage that makes them fearless and resistant to mind control during the fight.

RANGER

CAT
Quick, athletic, and has sharp claws.

GIANT WOLF SPIDER
Can spin webs, climb walls, and sneak around.

LIZARD
Quick, stealthy, and can give a nasty bite.

OWL
Able to fly, keen hearing and sight, and has sharp talons.

PANTHER
Sneaky, able to pounce, and has sharp claws and teeth.

RAT
Tiny and easily able to hide, can see in the dark, and has an annoying bite.

WOLF
Keen sense of smell and hearing, with a strong, powerful bite.

ANIMAL COMPANIONS

While some rangers prefer to be solitary hunters, many find friendships with animals in their travels, and some even form lasting fellowships with these animal allies. Here is a short list of possible animal companions.

BADGER
Quick, able to burrow, and has a sharp sense of smell.

BAT
Able to fly, can locate things in the dark, and has a keen sense of hearing.

BOAR
Can charge and attack with their sharp tusks.

Rangers are hunters, scouts, trappers, or nomads. They're warriors of the wilderness who specialize in stopping monsters that threaten civilization. Rangers feel comfortable in nature and can befriend local wildlife, but when it comes to taking down a specific target, they can be deadly and unrelenting.

In combat, rangers know how to use the immediate environment to their advantage. Any tree can be a hiding spot as they sneak up on their prey. Every field can be used to set a trap or snare. With practice, rangers learn how to wield simple nature spells to enhance their stealth, increase their speed, or strengthen their focused attacks.

EQUIPMENT AND ATTRIBUTES

Armor Rangers tend to wear light or medium armor (see pages 80 and 82) so they don't impede their movement or make too much noise.

Weapons Rangers prefer quick weapons to large and bulky ones. Swords, spears, knives, and axes in close combat and bows for ranged combat are the norm. Some rangers specialize in nonlethal capture of their prey, in which case they may use ropes, nets, snares, and even darts with mixtures that knock out their targets.

Favored Enemy Almost all rangers choose a type of monster on which to focus their hunting skills. Some rangers build their entire identity around hunting specific beasts— giant killers, dragon hunters, demon stalkers, or vampire slayers.

Natural Explorer Rangers may also specialize in making the most of a particular type of terrain: arctic, desert, forest, grassland, mountain, swamp, or the strange subterranean land known as the Underdark. Once the ranger enters their preferred environment, that training kicks in and they can be even more effective.

MINSC THE MIGHTY

PLAYING MINSC

Minsc is unwavering in his desire to battle evil and he will never back down from fighting for what he believes is good and right, even against enemies many times his size. He is fearlessly courageous, almost to the point of being suicidal. Everything Minsc does, he throws himself into with reckless abandon.

The legendary ranger is an eternal optimist, believing the best of himself, his allies, and everything around him. In Minsc's mind, the world is a very simple place of heroes and villains—either you're good or you're evil. Everyone he considers good should be his friend and everyone he considers evil needs a swift boot in the butt. Minsc's quest to prove he's a legendary hero never ends.

Minsc, and his hamster animal companion Boo, are fabled heroes known throughout a well-traveled part of the land called the Sword Coast. Over the years they have "kicked butt for goodness" many times, defeating monsters big and small while saving lives and building their reputation as great heroes.

The legendary ranger and his hamster are more than 100 years old thanks to an unexpected turn of events. During one of their adventures, the two were turned into a statue by evil magic and then, many decades later, turned back to flesh and blood. Minsc has always been a bit confused about where he is or who his friends are, and this bizarre time shift has only served to enhance his discombobulation.

BOO THE HAMSTER

Minsc is absolutely convinced that Boo is more than the small rodent he appears to be. Minsc tells his allies (and anyone else who will listen) that Boo is a "miniature giant space hamster," which sounds impressive but doesn't make a whole lot of sense. Whether or not Boo has this impressive lineage, he's definitely smarter than the average hamster and is capable of impressive problem solving. What's also apparent is that Boo is fiercely loyal to Minsc and, when things are dire, quite proficient at viciously fighting to defend his closest friend. An angry Boo will rapidly race around his opponent, biting, scratching, and attacking vital areas, including eyes, ears, the nose, and even "down below." Most enemies assume a hamster is not much of a threat, but a bum-bite from Boo quickly changes their minds.

ROGUE

DO YOU LIKE HIDING IN SHADOWS AND SURPRISING FRIENDS AND FOES?

ARE YOU SPEEDY INSTEAD OF STRONG?

IS YOUR MIND AS NIMBLE AS YOUR FINGERS?

YOU MIGHT MAKE A GOOD ROGUE!

THIEVES AND ASSASSINS When you have a reputation for sneaking around, picking locks, and going where you're not welcome, it's easy to see why common folk consider rogues as criminals. In many cases, they're not wrong. Many rogues break the law and take things that aren't theirs, but not all of them are evil. Some rogues do what they do for the thrill of adventure, enjoying the challenge of solving puzzles and exploring dangerous places.

Rogues are problem solvers. They rely on stealth and dexterity over big weapons and bigger muscles. When you need to get in somewhere without making a sound, pick a complex lock on a treasure chest, or set off a deadly trap without anyone getting hurt, you call in a rogue.

When it comes to combat, rogues rarely charge into battle. Remember, they're not fighters or paladins. A rogue would rather sneak up on a bad guy and make a precise strike that will impair the target. Successful rogues are versatile and resourceful, always looking for a solution that keeps them out of danger while getting them closer to filling their pouches with gleaming treasure.

EQUIPMENT AND ATTRIBUTES

Armor Rogues wear light armor (see page 80) so they can keep moving quickly while staying quiet.

Weapons Rogues tend to use small and fast weapons—daggers, rapiers, short swords, small crossbows, and so on. They value weapons that they can easily conceal and pull out at a moment's notice.

Sneak Attack Rogues specialize in distracting or surprising enemies in order to strike them in a vulnerable spot. In combat, rogues leave the loud and flashy attacks to their heavily armored friends while moving in from the sidelines like a cat ready to pounce at the perfect time.

Thieves' Cant Rogues have their own special form of communication. A combination of hand movements, facial expressions, symbols, and slang, it allows them to carry on a conversation without non-rogues knowing what they're really talking about. It's a good tool for gaining information in a seedy part of town or helping out a friend who shares the same profession.

SHANDIE FREEFOOT

TRICK SHOTS

Shandie's skill with a bow has reached such incredible levels that she can fire arrows into darkness and hit her target based solely on sound, or shoot into a windstorm and compensate for the violent changes in trajectory. Once Shandie sets her mind to hitting a target, her arrows almost always find their mark.

BOWYER AND FLETCHER

Shandie decided she didn't just want to master firing a bow, she wanted to understand every aspect of its creation. She studied how to craft her own bow from a single piece of wood and even whittle her own arrows. Controlling every part of the process has given Shandie even more confidence with her favorite weapon.

Shandie Freefoot is an infamous thief and archer based in Baldur's Gate, a coastal city with a reputation for secrets and scoundrels. She grew up on the rough and tumble streets of the Lower City and quickly learned that if she wanted to survive, she needed to be fast on her feet and even faster with her wit and weaponry. The first time Shandie saw a bowman gracefully launch an arrow into a bull's-eye, she knew she had to master archery. Halfling elders told her that her small size would make it too difficult to carry a bow and strike targets across a battlefield, but she took that as a challenge. With years of practice, Shandie learned how to rapidly climb to high vantage points and effortlessly fire arrows while constantly staying on the move. Any opponents underestimating this stealthy halfling rogue soon realize how dangerous she is as a volley of arrows bear down on them from unexpected rooftops or shadowy corners.

PLAYING SHANDIE Shandie is confident and cool under pressure. She's been through enough scrapes to know that she can figure a way out of almost any situation. Once she draws back an arrow and prepares to fire, she is completely focused, holding perfectly still while she decides how much speed and power she'll need to strike her target.

THE QUIVER OF EHLONNA

Over the course of her adventures, Shandie acquired a magical quiver. A regular quiver can hold approximately twenty arrows and weighs about 2 pounds. The Quiver of Ehlonna looks like a well-crafted piece of equipment, but few people realize it can hold up to sixty arrows in the exact same space and with the same weight as a normal quiver. When Shandie draws an arrow, the quiver magically replenishes, keeping her well stocked in combat and surprising foes who assume she's run out of ammunition.

CLASS FLOWCHART

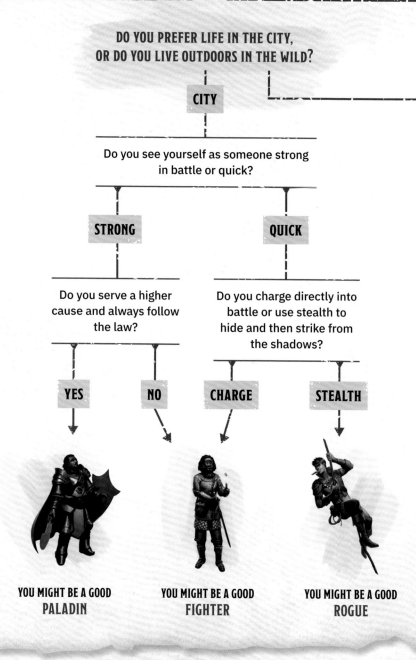

DO YOU PREFER LIFE IN THE CITY,
OR DO YOU LIVE OUTDOORS IN THE WILD?

CITY

Do you see yourself as someone strong
in battle or quick?

STRONG   **QUICK**

Do you serve a higher
cause and always follow
the law?

Do you charge directly into
battle or use stealth to
hide and then strike from
the shadows?

YES   **NO**   **CHARGE**   **STEALTH**

YOU MIGHT BE A GOOD
PALADIN

YOU MIGHT BE A GOOD
FIGHTER

YOU MIGHT BE A GOOD
ROGUE

Choosing a character class can be difficult, so here's
a little chart you can use to help you decide.

OUTDOORS

Do you see yourself as someone angry
in battle or more calm?

ANGRY

CALM

Do you launch a head-on
assault in battle, or are you
more strategic in order to
keep your opponent off guard?

Do you enjoy being in
nature and with animals, or
do you prefer to be alone
with your thoughts?

ASSAULT

STRATEGIC

NATURE

ALONE

YOU MIGHT BE A GOOD
BARBARIAN

YOU MIGHT BE A GOOD
RANGER

YOU MIGHT BE A GOOD
MONK

CHARACTER BACKGROUND & INSPIRATION

Characters are more than just their race or class; they're individuals with their own special stories to be told. You get to decide where your hero came from and how their experiences have led them to this point. Here are a few sample background ideas to help inspire your concept. You can use one of these or create your own.

ACOLYTE Your character was raised in a temple and knows the sacred rites and customs. Are you still friends with the church? Do you go on quests to raise funds for them?

CRIMINAL You've been a troublemaker for a long time and have struggled to stay on the right side of the law. Are you still committing crimes, or are you trying to mend your ways? Do you have criminal contacts who might still be looking for you?

ENTERTAINER You thrive when there's an audience in front of you looking for entertainment. What kind of performance do you specialize in—dance, music, poetry, singing, or something else? Are you just getting your start, or are you well-known for your art form?

FOLK HERO You may come from a small village or far-off town, but you're already starting to gain a reputation as a person who others look to in their time of need. What did you do in the past to gain this reputation? What heroic deeds are you hoping to achieve in the future?

HERMIT You've lived away from towns and cities for a long time, whether that was in a monastery or completely on your own somewhere remote. What has brought you back from your isolation? Are you excited to reconnect with the rest of the world, or do you want to get back to solitude as soon as possible?

NOBLE You have a title and your family owns land or riches. They may also have local political influence. Is your family well-liked by the locals, or do they have a bad reputation? Do you enjoy being part of this famous family, or do you hide your family name from those you meet?

OUTLANDER You've grown up away from large populations and you feel most comfortable in the wilderness. What do you think of city dwellers? How do you deal with people who destroy forests or mine the land?

SAGE You've always felt more comfortable reading books and studying scrolls. You have a lot of knowledge, but you've yet to put it into practice in the wider world. What has prompted you to leave your books and go on an adventure? How do you feel about war and conflict?

SOLDIER War has always been a part of your life, whether as part of a mercenary company or a recruit in a full-size army. Either way, you understand armed conflict and following orders. Are you still hungry for battle, or has your opinion changed? Did you earn rank in an army, or did you desert your post?

URCHIN You grew up on the streets, orphaned and poor. You learned to fend for yourself and survive, all the while yearning for something more. What was the name of the city you grew up in? Do you still have contacts there and, if so, how do they feel about you now?

DETAILS &
WHAT MAKES YOU SPECIAL

Once you've figured out your main features and where your character came from, it's time to work out the details that will make them unique and interesting.

NAME Names are important. They create an impression and build expectations. A powerful-sounding name, like "Battlehammer," tells people you're a capable warrior, while a name such as "Fenius" can sound mysterious or sly. Silly or serious, bubbly or brutal, whatever you choose, make sure it's something that exemplifies the key traits of your character.

HEIGHT AND WEIGHT
You don't need to work out your exact height and weight, but it can be useful to know which races tend to be taller than others.

Every hero has a distinctive element that helps them stand out from the crowd. It might be something internal, like a secret they keep or a piece of ancient lore they discovered, or it might be external, like a special birthmark, an item they carry, or an expertise they have. When coming up with ideas for your character, figure out what makes them special while not overlapping too much with other characters. Everyone in the group deserves to have their own unique feature.

Give your character a big goal to accomplish or a faraway place to visit and you'll see how easy it can be to build a story around their adventures.

OTHER PHYSICAL CHARACTERISTICS

You can decide if your character is young or old, as well as the color of their skin, hair, and eyes. Speaking of hair—how much of it do they have and how short or long do they keep it? Do they have any tattoos, scars, or other markings?

Close your eyes and imagine how your character might look. The more distinctive and interesting you can make them, the better.

DON'T FORGET FLAWS

It may seem counterintuitive when you're creating someone heroic, but adding weaknesses can help make someone distinctive. It's fun to think about flaws and make them part of your character's personality.

Is your character afraid of something? Do they have something they hate? Are they dimwitted, quick tempered, disorganized, or scatterbrained? Are they allergic to cats, loose with their money, or do they have an old injury that gives them a hard time?

Give your character at least one flaw and you might be surprised at how enjoyable it can be to incorporate it into their history.

HATS

Headgear is available in a wide range of styles and sizes, from close-fitting rogue caps to huge, floppy wizard hats. Whatever the design, they're helpful for keeping sun and rain off the faces of weary adventurers trekking from dungeon to dungeon.

CLOAK

Part clothing, part blanket, a cloak is crucial for protecting you from bad weather, concealing you from enemies, and keeping you warm at night.

SHIRT

Some adventurers prefer loose shirts for mobility, and others like a more fitted garment that won't impede them while fighting. Either way, shirts can range from plain and rough to ultra-soft items made from the finest fabrics.

WAISTCOAT

Waistcoats are worn for reasons of warmth, style, and all those extra little pockets.

PANTS/SKIRT

Either pants or skirts are suitable for adventuring, so long as they are made from sturdy fabric and cut loose enough to allow a full range of movement. You can wear a skirt over leggings for added warmth.

FOOTWEAR

Boots are the most common footwear choice for adventurers, helping to protect your lower legs from water, slime, and ankle-biting beasts. Some adventurers prefer a soft-soled shoe that allows for extra-quiet footsteps.

CLOTHES: ANATOMY OF AN ADVENTURER'S OUTFIT

Clothing can say a lot about your character's personality, wealth, and social status. In turn, that affects how other characters, including allies and villains, respond to you. Fancy robes can help during negotiations with a local lord—or help you infiltrate that same lord's castle on a secret mission. Many magic users prefer long, loose garments with lots of hidden storage spots for their spell components and enchanted talismans. Some vestments are even covered with symbolic or magical designs. The tattered rags of a peasant might cause a warlock to hesitate when trusting you with an important quest—or allow you to pass through a crowd unnoticed by soldiers who are searching for you.

TRINKETS

Carried usually for sentimental reasons, trinkets are small objects that reflect your character's background and personality but aren't useful in combat (unless you're very creative!). They can also play a role in your interactions with other characters or provide the spark of inspiration for stories. Ideas include:

- A crystal that glows faintly in the moonlight
- A coin from an unknown land
- A tiny knife that belonged to a relative
- An empty vial that smells of perfume when opened

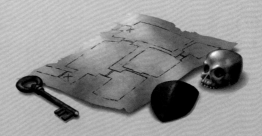

WHAT TO WEAR WHEN YOU'RE ADVENTURING!

Your choice of clothing can change how you move, how you fight, and how others interact with you. What you wear changes your style and strategy, so choose carefully.

THE CLASS MAKES THE CLOTHES!

Although adventurers are free to wear whatever they like, each class does lean toward certain types of clothing that best suits their abilities.

- **Barbarian** These fierce, primitive warriors prefer garments that maximize their ability to move quickly and inflict damage on their enemies. They value durability over decoration, although many carry tokens of their home tribes on their adventures.

- **Fighter** Highly trained combat specialists, the clothing of these classic warriors ranges from plain materials to colorful displays of their sworn allegiances.

- **Monk** Masters of the martial arts, these spiritual warriors rely solely on their body's defenses, favoring plain monastic robes that allow their ki to flow freely.

- **Paladin** These holy warriors prefer standard adventurer's garb, and they often incorporate symbols of their faith into their attire.

- **Ranger** These nature-based trackers and hunters favor muted shades that let them blend in to their forest environments.

- **Rogue** Stealth is important to rogues, who favor dark colors and garb that lets them move quiet and unseen through the world.

ADVENTURER'S CLOTHES

Durable clothes created to survive the varied dangers of a dungeon environment, including the cold and damp, or battle damage. Designed to be easily repaired, and often given a personal touch to help bolster an adventurer's spirit.

Wear this when trekking into dangerous environments—or to impress locals with tales of your past adventures.

Don't wear this when you need to stay out of sight. Adventurers attract attention, and not always the friendly kind.

FINE CLOTHES

Ornate attire made from expensive materials, which may even feature silk threads and gemstone decorations.

Wear this when you need to impress nobles, engage in diplomacy, or intimidate poor folks.

Don't wear this when you're out adventuring—fancy fabrics are too delicate for the dangers of a dungeon, and all that bling may attract nasty creatures!

TRAVELER'S CLOTHES

Sturdy, practical clothing in rough, but durable, fabric. Often features long cloaks for warmth and protection against the elements!

Wear this when you're traveling long distances or trying to find a spot at an inn.

Don't wear this to a fancy banquet, unless you want to upset your host.

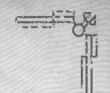

EQUIPMENT

The right equipment is of paramount importance to an adventurer. The proper gear can mean the difference between life and death when trapped in a dungeon or while traveling across rugged lands. Weapons and armor seem obvious, but what about the other things you might need? Rope to climb steep cliffs and lockpicks to open sealed doors, a tinderbox to start fires and a bedroll to sleep on, a lantern to guide you through the dark and rations to keep you fed. You can't carry *everything*—that'd be far too heavy—so you'll need to pack carefully!

As you create your character, think about their background and where their equipment—or the gold to buy it—came from. Are you the only child of wealthy merchants, able to afford the best of everything, or did you come from humble beginnings, earning your gear through hard work and careful saving? Do you wear robes unique to the monastery where you were raised or possess a legendary axe inherited from a famous relative? Your equipment helps tell the story of who your character was before their adventure began and bolsters victory in your upcoming quests!

WEAPONS:
BE READY FOR
COMBAT

Whether you favor a longsword or a longbow, your weapon and your ability to use it effectively while adventuring will mean the difference between life and death. Your race and class can make you extra-effective with certain weapons or prevent you from using others, so you'll want to take both into consideration when making your choices.

Most people can use simple weapons without needing extra training. These include clubs, maces, and other arms often found in the hands of common folks. Martial weapons, including swords, axes, and polearms, require more specialized training. It's possible to injure yourself instead of an enemy if you attack with a weapon you don't know how to use, so watch out!

In addition to functionality, you should think about personal touches that make your weapons cool and unique. Is your axe engraved with dwarven runes? Does your dagger have a jeweled handle or a special scabbard? Was your shortbow's wood hewn from a sacred tree in far-off elvish lands? Your weapon will be your constant companion on the adventure ahead, so choose one you can trust!

SWORDS

The classic warriors' weapon, swords are made from a long piece of metal sharpened on both edges and mounted on a sturdy handle known as a hilt. They come in a range of lengths and weights and may be highly decorated or left plain, depending on the owner's wealth and taste.

Swords can be used to slash at enemies, puncture them with the sharp tip, and even deliver blunt strikes with the broadside or the hilt. The more ways your warrior can think of to wield their weapon, the harder it will be for enemies to dodge their attacks!

SHORTSWORD
Nimble and adaptable, shortswords are popular across most character classes. Their light weight makes them a great choice for long journeys, and their lower cost makes them a popular option for adventurers who are just starting out.

As a one-handed weapon, shortswords allow their user to carry a shield as well—an important consideration for warriors who are restricted from some of the tougher armor classes. Don't underestimate the damage a skilled hero can do with one of these swift, sharp implements at their side!

LONGSWORD
The versatile longsword offers a great balance between the speed of a shortsword and the hefty power of a greatsword. As a one-handed weapon, they permit a hero to deliver swift, sharp strikes while allowing for a shield as extra protection. Used with both hands, longswords focus the full brunt of a warrior's strength into punishing blows.

The longsword is a great choice when you're not certain what kind of danger you'll be facing. Whether you tangle with lots of smaller opponents who need to be taken down quickly or a mighty beast that can only be defeated with powerful hits, the longsword is ready to deliver!

GREATSWORD
The greatsword is a mighty weapon requiring immense strength and skill to use effectively. Any untrained heroes may wind up hurting themselves more than their opponents if they wade into battle with one of these!

A two-handed weapon, greatswords can deliver powerful blows, even killing lesser creatures with a single strike. Due to their size and expense, greatswords are associated with paladins, fighters, and barbarians, although any trained warrior with sufficient might may find one to be a welcome ally on the field of battle!

POLEARMS

Polearms consist of a staff, typically made of wood, topped with a metal spike or blade. A classic battlefield weapon, their broad reach makes them a great choice against larger opponents. Armies often place rows of soldiers armed with polearms as their first line of defense against attacking cavalry, goblin hordes, giants, and other foes.

As close-combat weapons, polearms' longer length allows a wider swing than swords, increasing your range and building speed for a more brutal impact. Combined with a steady stance, a polearm can deliver crushing blows; paired with nimble footwork, the blade becomes a flashing blur of stabs and slashes. What fighting style will your warrior choose?

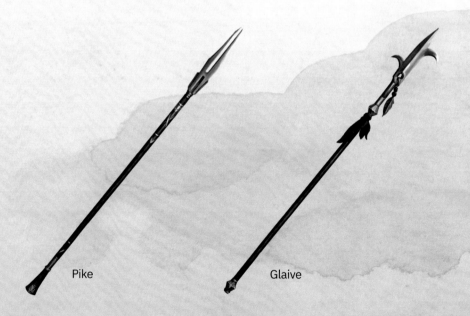

Pike

Glaive

PIKE Simple and effective, an inexpensive pike is a great weapon choice for starting heroes who find themselves short on gold. The spike delivers sharp stabbing damage to enemies, and can even be thrown if needed.

GLAIVE The curved hook of a glaive allows it to deal extra damage. You can even use it to snare opponents and pull them in close! The sharp edge of the blade can be used to stab or slash at foes for even more attack options.

HALBERD Combining the reach of a pike with the blade of an axe, a halberd opens up even more fighting techniques for a trained warrior. By gripping the staff near the base, you gain a wider range for your slashes, while holding it closer to the blade will deliver blows with a mighty impact.

FANG TIAN JI The complex blade of a fang tian ji is best placed in the hands of a highly trained fighter, for it takes years of experience to master the many attacks this weapon can achieve. Stabbing, slashing, even blunt impact from the flat side of the blade, this weapon will give you countless ways to overcome your foes.

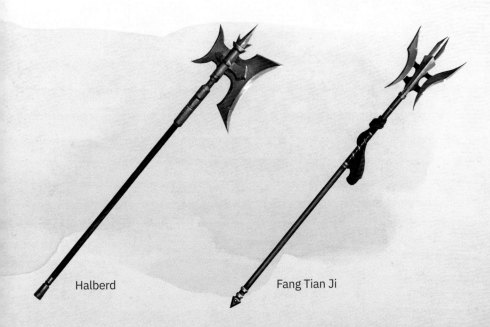

Halberd

Fang Tian Ji

OTHER MELEE WEAPONS

Swords and polearms are common choices of weapons for adventurers who like to get close to the enemy, but other options are available, including axes, hammers, and whips! These weapons are often very simple, but also very effective.

AXES Originally intended to cut down trees and split wood, axes first became a popular weapon among forest-dwellers. Axes range greatly in size and style. Some have one blade, and some have two; a pickaxe has a blade on one side and a pick on the other.

Hand axes can be used as both melee and thrown weapons, and some adventurers learn how to wield two hand axes at once! Most axes are still primarily tools, but some of the most stylish axes, like the long-handled pole axe, are designed specifically as weapons.

FLAILS
Flails were originally farmers' tools used to beat grain for harvesting, but farmers adapted them as weapons to defend against attackers. Basic flails consist of two wooden batons linked by a chain or rope. Sophisticated versions might include a blade, a metal claw, or a spiked metal ball on one or both ends. Martial artists may train all their lives to master the use of a flail.

HAMMERS
Intended as tools for construction, demolition, and metalwork, hammers have become favored weapons among some of the hardiest races, including orcs and dwarfs, since they offer brutal power.

Hammers range in size from modest sledge hammers to huge iron mauls. Many are basic blunt instruments for striking enemies or denting armor, but warhammers are designed as impressive smashing weapons with long handles and small heavy heads to be wielded with speed and grace.

MACES
Related to hammers, but conceived specifically as weapons, maces are metal bludgeons with spikes or blades designed to penetrate armor or pull a soldier off a horse. Because maces can be very ornate, they are sometimes the blunt weapon of choice for people of high status— but they can also be made from cheap raw iron and hit just as hard!

WHIPS
Traditionally used for wrangling livestock, whips can be used as weapons by a highly trained expert. Some bullwhips extend as far as twenty feet, offering greater range than most melee weapons!

Other styles of whip have less reach but different advantages. Scourges are whips with multiple short tails that can be used to disarm an opponent. A riding crop can be carried discretely and delivers a stinging blow rather than lasting damage. Chain whips, made of metal rods linked by chains, are less flexible than other whips, but they hit very hard.

RANGED WEAPONS

Most ranged weapons were originally intended for hunting, but in a world of spellcasters, firebreathers, and terrible flying beasts, the ability to attack at long range can be a lifesaver. Bows and arrows are the most popular forms of ranged weapons, but they come in a few different styles, and there are some ranged weapons that might prove a better fit for your character.

BOWS Shortbows and longbows use the tension of a bowstring released by hand to propel an arrow toward a target. Shortbows are about three feet in height and can fire an arrow about eighty feet on average. Longbows are a couple of feet taller and can typically fire an arrow about one hundred fifty feet, but they're not as easy to carry around. All bows require some strength to use effectively.

CROSSBOWS Crossbows are simple mechanical weapons activated by pulling a trigger to release a catch on the bowstring, propelling a bolt toward a target. There are three popular types.

Hand crossbows are small and can be fired one-handed, but have a usual range of about thirty feet, and the string must be drawn back by hand. Light crossbows and heavy crossbows must be held two-handed, and a crank or lever is used to pull back the string. Light crossbows have a range of eighty feet, while a large and weighty heavy crossbow has a range of one hundred feet. Most crossbows can only fire one bolt at a time, and reloading can take several minutes.

DARTS (BLOW DARTS) Piercing darts can be thrown about twenty feet or shot from a blowgun to a distance of about twenty-five feet. Darts don't deliver much damage, so they are often tipped with dangerous or deadly poisons to make them more effective.

SLINGS A simple projectile weapon made of a pouch and cord, slings are used to fling a small blunt projectile with great force an average of thirty feet. Hard metal projectiles called "bullets" are often used, but one great advantage of a sling is that they can also launch found objects such as rocks or even coins!

THROWING WEAPONS Daggers, shurikens, and other bladed throwing weapons have a range of twenty to thirty feet, depending on their weight and design. They require great finesse and aim to use effectively.

SPECIAL WEAPONS

If a sword or axe isn't your style, there are other options to consider. A unique "signature weapon" that matches your fighting style or history is one way your character might stand out from other adventurers.

BOOMERANG A thrown hunting weapon made of wood or bone that delivers a bludgeoning strike to a target. Expert users can throw a boomerang so that it returns to their hand, but only if it hasn't struck a target.

CHAIN Heavy iron chains are challenging weapons to wield, but if you have the strength to haul and swing a length of chain, you can hit hard!

NET Weighted fishing nets can be hurled at opponents, tangling them up and leaving them vulnerable to follow-up attacks.

PICK A small, sharp spike with a handle, traditionally used for breaking up ice or stone. Easily concealed, and effective in close-quarters combat.

PUSH DAGGER Another easily concealed close-quarters weapon, comprising a small stabbing blade and a horizontal handle that rests in the user's palm.

SCYTHE Originally designed for harvesting crops, scythes are long-handled tools with a curved horizontal blade used in a sweeping motion. Difficult to use as a weapon, but the blade can be reforged for use on a polearm or sword.

SICKLE A small one-handed version of a scythe. Its curved blade makes it a great choice for martial artists who strike at unexpected angles.

TRIDENT A spear with three prongs designed for spear fishing. A trident can be used as a throwing or thrusting weapon.

CRAZY COMBINATIONS

Instead of choosing a special weapon, you might take two familiar weapons and combine them in unusual ways. The only limits are your imagination! Here are some examples.

Dagger + Rope If you're an expert at throwing a dagger, adding a rope allows you to yank the dagger back.

Chain + Hammer A weighted chain with a bludgeon on the end creates an effective weapon for sweeping your enemies off their feet.

Crossbow + Axe Adding an axe blade to a crossbow creates a weapon that can be used for both ranged and melee combat.

Spear + Scythe Combining a spear and a scythe on either side of a pole creates a more versatile weapon for both forward and sideways attacks. Just remember to always check behind you!

Sword + Staff A sword can be hidden inside a staff or stick, giving you more options in combat and a chance to deliver a nasty surprise!

ARMOR: THE FOUNDATION OF A HERO'S DEFENSE

The toughest armor isn't always the best defense. Too much armor can slow down your character or even interfere with their magical abilities. Too little armor can leave you vulnerable to damage, especially if you tend to get up close and personal in a fight. Remember that some classes have restrictions on what kinds of armor they can use, so check what's available before you set your heart on that shiny suit of plate mail. Choose carefully if you want to survive the dangers ahead!

Budget is also a consideration for starting characters. Fancy metal armor can eat up all your savings, leaving you without the coins you'll need for food and additional gear. On the other hand, that homemade hide suit may be cheap, but it also won't offer much protection in a real fight. There's always a balance to be found when selecting armor.

GETTING IN (AND OUT) OF YOUR ARMOR

Putting on armor is no easy task. The speed with which you can go from normal clothes to full protection depends on the weight of your armor.

- **Light Armor** One minute
- **Medium Armor** Five minutes
- **Heavy Armor** Ten minutes

Make Your Choice Do you want to sit up for your turn keeping night watch in heavy, uncomfortable armor? Or, take the risk of having nothing but your weapon to protect you if there's an ambush? Luckily, it takes only a second to grab your trusty shield!

LIGHT ARMOR

Made from lightweight and flexible materials, light armor is the best choice for nimble adventurers. It will reduce damage from minor blows but might not be enough to protect you from stronger opponents.

PADDED ARMOR

Made from quilted layers of cloth and batting, padded armor is lightweight and affordable, but not very strong. Be warned: This simple armor is bulky, which means your character is less stealthy than normal while wearing it.

Not ideal if you want to stay unnoticed.

LEATHER ARMOR

The chest and shoulders of this armor are made of stiffened leather boiled in oil to increase its strength. The rest is made from softer materials that won't interfere with movement.

A great compromise between protection and weight, and pretty affordable too.

STUDDED LEATHER ARMOR

This is leather armor that has been reinforced with rivets and spikes to help deflect blows.

Be careful, though—this type of armor is a lot more expensive than normal leather armor, and a lot heavier too. You don't want to wear this on a long trek unless you're quite strong.

CHOOSE WISELY

Remember, the more protection an armor provides, the more it interferes with your ability to move freely. If your character relies on being quick and agile, too much armor can actually be a bad thing.

MEDIUM ARMOR

Willing to sacrifice some mobility for extra protection? Medium armor may be just what you need. It's ideal for those who like to get into the thick of battle but possess more skills than just straightforward smashing to help them win the day.

HIDE Fit for a barbarian, this crude armor consists of thick furs and pelts that wrap around the body. Many evil humanoids also favor this type of protection.

CHAIN SHIRT
Made of interlocking rings, a chain shirt provides modest protection. It's great at deflecting sharp blades, but less helpful against bashing damage from maces or hammers. Its rings can be loud when they clink together, so to muffle the noise it's best worn as a layer between your regular clothing and a leather outer shell.

SCALE MAIL
This armor is a mixture of leather and metal pieces overlapping like the scales of a fish—hence its name. With a coat, leggings, gloves, and sometimes an overskirt, it provides full-body protection for the intrepid adventurer.

BREASTPLATE
Combining the solid toughness of a metal torso with the flexibility of leather armor, a breastplate helps protect your vital organs without weighing you down too much. Be careful, though, your chest may be safe, but your arms and legs are still exposed.

HALF PLATE
Covering most of the wearer's body, these shaped metal plates are held together by leather straps to ensure the armor stays in place throughout the toughest fight. This type of armor is very strong but does have open gaps that leave weak spots for a skilled opponent to target.

HEAVY ARMOR

This tough stuff is your best bet for getting through a rough fight unscathed. However, the weight and bulk of heavy armor means that only the strongest and most experienced of warriors can wear it in combat without encountering speed or movement difficulties.

RING MAIL This is leather armor with heavy rings stitched across the surface. Metal makes it heavy to wear, but it's not as protective as chain mail because its rings are more spread out. On the plus side, it's less expensive than chain, making it a thrifty choice for beginning adventurers.

CHAIN MAIL The interlocking metal rings over a layer of quilted fabric in this armor provides solid protection against sharp-edged weapons such as swords and arrows. Be careful, though, you can still bruise beneath chain mail, and the tiny rings can be noisy when moving around!

SPLINT ARMOR Thin metal strips riveted onto leather backing create this tough, durable armor. Chain mail is added at the joints for extra protection at flexible spots, while thick padded fabric underneath keeps your skin from chafing.

PLATE MAIL The classic armor of knights and adventurers, this huge metal suit is designed to provide protection from head to toe. You'll need thick padding underneath to protect your skin, and well-fashioned straps to keep the weight properly aligned over your whole body. And plate armor is loud, so forget sneaking up on most creatures while wearing this.

SHIELDS

Often, a shield is an adventurer's best friend. Capable of stopping a wide range of attacks, from swords and arrows to warhammers and whips, shields are quick and versatile defensive tools. You can even use them as a bludgeoning weapon if you're backed into a corner and disarmed.

SHIELD MATERIAL AND PARTS
Shields are made from many different materials, including wood, hardened leather, and metal. Wood and leather shields may have metal parts, like edges or spikes, to enhance their durability.

UMBO
A raised metal circle placed at the center of some shields, the umbo helps deflect blows aimed at the middle of the shield.

ENARMES
Leather-wrapped gripping handle attached to the back of the shield.

GUIGE
The long leather strap used to carry the shield across your back.

BUCKLER A small, round shield designed for basic personal protection, bucklers tend to be lightweight, inexpensive, and easy to carry and use. Their versatile design makes them the most common of all shields.

KITE Wide at the top and narrow at the bottom, kites are a longer shield that provides more coverage than a buckler. You can drive the pointed edge into the ground for added stability against an assault.

HEATER A smaller variation of the kite, a heater often has a peaked top to help defect sword blows. Its base is a little wider, giving more protection to the upper legs but potentially leaving your calves open to attack.

IMPROVISED Almost any object can become a shield with enough ingenuity—or desperation! Loose doors, coffin lids, metal serving plates, almost anything that's sturdy and in reach can help protect you from an enemy attack. You don't even need to be able to lift it—an overturned table or treasure chest makes a great place to hide from arrows! What kinds of improvised shields can you think of?

RUST MONSTER

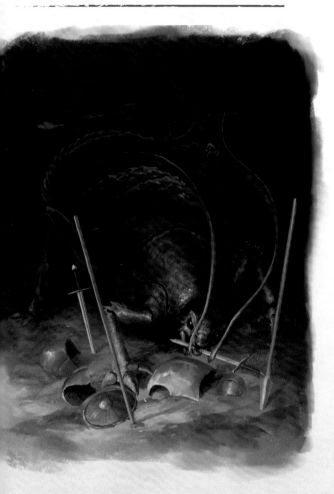

LAIR Rust monsters live underground, scavenging for weapons left in dungeons by unwary adventurers who have met an untimely end. They're often found near larger and more formidable creatures, because those beasts tend to generate a lot of scrap metal from the adventurers they eat! Thankfully, rust monsters rarely travel in large packs.

SPECIAL POWERS

SENSE METAL
Because rust monsters feed exclusively on metal, they can perceive ferrous metals up to fifty feet away. Single-minded in their pursuit of food, they may attack anyone who gets between them and dinner.

CORROSION
Rust monsters can corrode ferrous metals they touch and will destroy any vulnerable weapons used to attack them. The effects of their corrosion are irreversible, though some magical weapons and armors are immune to their powers.

SIZE Rust monsters resemble fleas, but you'll never find one on a dog. They're big enough to send most dogs running in the other direction! A fully grown rust monster is four to six feet long and weighs about 300 pounds.

The flealike giant insectoids called rust monsters are a terrible sight to encounter in the subterranean caverns they call home, but they're much more of a threat to your arms and armor than they are to you! Rust monsters feed on ferrous metals, which are any metals containing iron and vulnerable to rusting. That includes iron, steel, adamantine, and mithral.

There are much more dangerous creatures out there than these beasts (enough to fill a whole other book), but losing your equipment to a rust monster can leave you vulnerable to the next danger you encounter. For many adventurers, a run-in with a rust monster must be avoided at all costs, especially if said adventurers managed to buy or acquire the finest weapons available! Being very proud of their own ironwork, dwarves particularly hate rust monsters!

Some people keep rust monsters as pets—like a guard dog that's very effective against heavily armed intruders—but they need to be well fed, or they'll turn on your defenses!

DO THIS

Always carry at least one weapon that can't rust. A rust monster's hide is well-armored, so make sure the weapon you use is a tough one.

Dump your least valuable iron items in a rust monster's path. This may distract it as you run away. Many cooking pots have been lost in this manner.

DON'T DO THIS

Don't attack rust monsters. If you're not carrying any ferrous metals, they will happily ignore you.

Don't ever use your best iron or steel weapons to attack them. That is, unless those weapons are enchanted!

IN YOUR PACK: ITEMS FOR TRAVEL & EXPLORATION

Being a dungeon delver requires courage, a desire to explore, and the right tools for the challenges ahead. What you carry determines your success against tough terrain, worrisome weather, and creepy creatures.

Adventuring packs are an easy way to get all the gear you need for a particular task or quest, usually at lower cost than buying all the equipment individually. Your character class will probably inform the kind of starting equipment you'll want to take on your journey, and these packs might be just what you're looking for.

Even so, you can't take it all. Getting packed for an epic journey means making choices about what to bring and what to leave behind. Every bit of equipment or weaponry can slow you down, tire you out, or leave less room to carry the treasures you may find during your travels.

Use the information in this chapter to make a list of what you want to carry based on your class and its abilities, then outfit your heroic self and head toward adventure!

SURVIVAL GEAR

Whether crossing a desert, navigating a forest, or delving deep into a dungeon, there are certain things every adventurer needs to prepare for if they hope to survive, and that means bringing the right gear.

SHELTER The most basic form of shelter is a bedroll and a blanket but, if you can carry it, a weatherproof tarpaulin will help protect you from the elements. Better yet, bring a tent. Of course, some races are fine curling up in a tree or digging themselves a hole in the ground.

WATER A good waterskin is a vital piece of equipment for any adventurer, and you should take every opportunity to top up with clean drinkable water from a spring or stream.

FIRE Another vital piece of equipment is a tinderbox to light fires to keep you warm at night, cook food and boil water, and perhaps keep predators at bay. A tinderbox contains steel and flint, which can be struck together to create sparks, and some form of tinder, like wooden kindling or a flammable cloth, which can be used to ignite a fire.

LIGHT If you're navigating underground or by night, you'll need torches made from sticks wrapped in oil cloths that can be lit from a fire. Many adventuring races have darkvision, allowing them to see in low light, but this ability won't allow you to see colors in the dark.

FOOD Adventure food needs to be compact and durable. Hardtack biscuits, made with just flour and water, are a popular choice. These crackers keep for a very long time but taste terribly plain. If you can't pack enough food for a long journey or want something flavorful, hunting and fishing equipment are very useful, so long as you know what to do with them! A guidebook to safe foraging is also helpful, plus a cooking pot in which to prepare your meals.

NAVIGATION A magnetic compass will help you find your way through unfamiliar territory, though remember that iron-rich caverns can throw off its accuracy. If a map exists for where you're going, it's a good idea to bring that too.

FIRST AID A basic healer's kit contains bandages, lotions, and splints, all of which are very useful if you forgot to bring a healer for your party—or if your healer is the one injured!

ADVENTURING GEAR

Defeat the monster, get the gold, avenge the people, save the day—adventuring is about more than just survival. Getting past every obstacle and facing off against every threat requires special equipment, so acquiring the right adventuring gear is very important.

Adventuring gear is just about anything that might help you get to your goal, aside from weapons, armor, trinkets, and magical items. These are some of the most popular examples.

Climber's Kit + Rope

AMMUNITION If your weapon of choice is a sling, a bow, or a blowgun, make sure you pack enough shots, arrows, bolts, or darts for the journey.

BALL BEARINGS The thief's favorite. A handful of ball bearings tossed on flat ground can create an instant tripping obstacle for anyone chasing after you!

CLIMBER'S KIT Whether you're scaling a cliff, a tree, or a castle wall, you'll be safer with a climbing kit that includes pitons, gloves, and a harness.

Component Pouch

COMPONENT POUCH A leather pouch that hangs from your belt, with separate compartments to hold the items needed for a spell.

Hunting Trap

HUNTING TRAP A heavy iron trap that you can set on the ground to catch big beasts (or unwary foes).

POTION OF HEALING Never leave home without it!

ROPE Rope is very useful for climbing, but you can also use it for setting traps, swinging across a chasm, or tying up prisoners.

Potion of Healing

TOOLS

Whether you're picking locks, mixing potions, or performing for a crowd, you need the right tools for the job—and you need to know how to use them.

Tools are ordinary items associated with a craft, trade, or hobby. If you're playing a character who is supposed to be particularly good at a task, whether it's an honest woodworker or a cunning thief, you'll want to make sure you have the proper equipment.

Tools are often available in sets based around a profession. You should assume they contain everything you need to do that job, but none of the raw materials. For example, herbalist kits include a mortar and pestle, clippers, and pouches, but no plants. Jeweler kits include tiny pliers, hammers, and clamps, but no jewels.

POPULAR TOOL SETS

Alchemist's Supplies Includes a mortar and pestle, vials, flasks, and measuring spoons, so you can attempt to mix up potions or create precious metals.

Carpenter's Tools Includes hammers, saws, chisels, levels, and nails, but you'll have to fetch your own wood.

Cook's Utensils Includes a cooking pot, a pan, knives, and wooden spoons, as well as bowls to serve in. If you know how to use these items, you'll never be lonely on an adventure!

Disguise Kit Includes hair dye, makeup, and props to help you disguise or conceal your appearance.

Forgery Kit Includes papers, inks, and sealing wax to allow you to create convincing fake documents.

Gaming Set Includes dice, playing cards, and other game pieces that you can use to make friends—or enemies—in a local tavern.

Mapmaker's Tools Includes parchments, measuring tools, and inks, so you can always keep track of where you've been.

Musical Instruments Essential for every bard, whether it's a simple flute or a set of bagpipes.

Thief's Tools Includes lock picks, files, pliers, and a long-handled mirror. Great for opening locks and disabling traps!

BURGLAR'S PACK

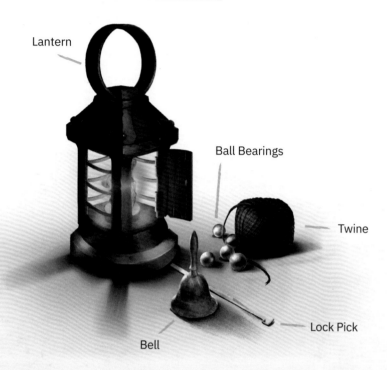

Lantern

Ball Bearings

Twine

Lock Pick

Bell

Burglars will tell you that what they do is an art; they're not just opportunistic thieves or rough hoodlums. They choose a target and go in quietly, taking only what they need and leaving the scene as undisturbed as possible.

A burglar's pack contains many of the essential tools of the trade, including a lantern that can be covered quickly, a bell that can be attached to twine to warn of passing patrols, a lot of rope, some ball bearings, and a crowbar and hammer for cracking locks. Of course, expert burglars may leave those last two behind if they know how to use a set of lock picks.

DUNGEONEER'S PACK

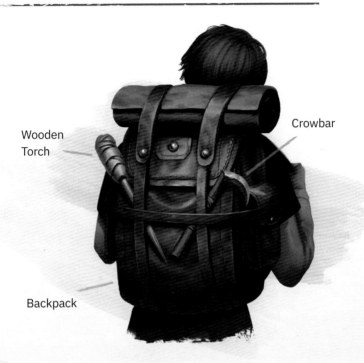

Wooden
Torch

Crowbar

Backpack

You'll hopefully encounter a lot more dungeons than dragons in your adventures, and a dungeoneering pack contains the basic equipment for venturing down into the dark in search of treasure, including a backpack, a tinderbox, rope, climbing pitons, hardtack biscuits, a waterskin, and a crowbar and hammer.

One of the most important items in your dungeoneering pack is a set of wooden torches. Set one on fire, and you'll have a light to see by, helping you navigate traps and search for treasure. Of course, torches might also give away your location if anyone else happens to be watching.

EXPLORER'S PACK

Waterskin

Bedroll

Cup

Square Tin

Rations

Tinderbox

Any adventurer may be called upon to endure a long journey while fulfilling a quest, but those who have chosen the life of an explorer are especially well prepared for travel.

An explorer's pack includes a backpack, a bedroll, torches, a tinderbox, a waterskin, and some rope, plus a mess kit for preparing and eating food, which usually includes a square tin, a cup, and cutlery. The pack will also include several days' worth of rations.

VAMPIRE HUNTER'S PACK

Holy Water

Holy Symbols

Wooden Stakes

Mallet

Mirror

Vampires are incredibly dangerous creatures with a frightening array of occult abilities, and experienced vampire hunters may spend years developing the perfect set of tools to fight these monsters.

Of course, even an apprentice vampire hunter will be given the essentials, usually in a beautifully crafted wooden chest. These include wooden stakes and a mallet, which is used to drive a stake into a vampire's heart, plus a mirror to help detect the fiends, and holy water and holy symbols, sacred to their own particular god, to chase the wretches away.

USING HEROES
TO TELL YOUR OWN STORIES

Growling sounds and the scrape of steel against steel echoed around the broken statues and other debris in the chamber. Six goblins wielding notched spears and rusty swords moved toward Whey-Shu from all sides.

The kenku monk waited. She was not the type to make the first move in battle. The dark feathers all over her body quivered slightly from the movement of the air, but she was otherwise absolutely still. It was better to size up her opponents and look for flaws in their combat technique than to recklessly charge forth into close combat too soon.

The largest of the goblins, clearly the pack leader, spoke with a snarl.

"Surrender, little bird, or we'll clip your wings."

Whey-Shu knew that even if she did give up, they would never let her leave this place alive. She also knew that goblins were impulsive creatures. If they were hesitating instead of charging immediately at her, then it must be because they knew who she was and feared what she was capable of.

Perhaps this would be a worthy challenge after all. . . .

Reading about adventure is a great way to stir your imagination, and creating a character is an important first step in composing your personal stories. Building a new character is about discovering who they are at the beginning of their journey and then figuring out who they might become as their legend grows across the land.

Your idea might start with a single hero or a small group of adventurers, but it can go *anywhere*: a creature's lair, the village nearby, cities and dungeons, caverns or skyscapes. You get to choose all the ingredients and stir them together. To help you as you develop your story, here are some questions to keep in mind:

WHO ARE YOUR CHARACTERS?

- Are your heroes like you or different? Young or old, human or something else? Think about the foes you must face. Great heroes require great challenges. What makes your villains memorable and powerful, and what brings them into conflict with your adventurers?

WHERE DOES YOUR STORY TAKE PLACE?

- At the top of a mountain, in a serene forest, deep underwater, or in a creepy boneyard?

WHEN DOES THE STORY HAPPEN?

- At night or during the day, in the middle of a thunderstorm or right before the bells toll to ring in the new year? Think about time passing as your story unfolds.

HOW DO THINGS CHANGE AS THE STORY PROCEEDS?

- Do your heroes succeed or fail? Do they find somewhere new or explore someplace old?

WHAT SHOULD SOMEONE FEEL AS THEY EXPERIENCE YOUR STORY?

- Do you want them to laugh or get scared? Cheer or be grossed out?

WHY ARE YOUR HEROES GOING ON THIS ADVENTURE?

- Knowing what their goals are will help you create a compelling tale of courage and exploration.

Remember, you don't have to answer all these questions by yourself! DUNGEONS & DRAGONS is a collaborative game where you work with your friends to create your own stories. One person acts as a narrator, called a Dungeon Master, and the other players each take on the role of a hero, called a Player Character, in the adventuring party in a story. The Dungeon Master sets up a scene by describing a place and any threats that may exist, and then each player contributes ideas by explaining their own character's actions. With each scene created by the group, the story moves forward in unexpected and entertaining ways.

If you don't feel confident starting from scratch, you can go to your local gaming store and play a DUNGEONS & DRAGONS demonstration session. Demos can be a quick way to learn how the game is played and an opportunity to possibly make some brand-new friends at the same time.

After you've read through all the character options in this little heroic handbook, there's even more DUNGEONS & DRAGONS material to ignite your imagination. The *Monsters & Creatures* guide is bursting at the seams with beasts and critters for you and your friends to discover. You know who your hero is and have equipped them for their journey, now find our what dangers lurk in the darkness and *answer the call to adventure*!

Published in the United States by Ten Speed Press, an imprint of Random House, a division of Penguin Random House LLC, New York.
www.crownpublishing.com
www.tenspeed.com

Ten Speed Press and the Ten Speed Press colophon are registered trademarks of Penguin Random House LLC.

Originally published in the United States in hardcover by Ten Speed Press, an imprint of Random House, a division of Penguin Random House LLC, New York, in 2019.

Publisher: Aaron Wehner
Art Director and Designer: Betsy Stromberg
Editors: Patrick Barb and Julie Bennett
Managing Editor: Doug Ogan
Production Designer: Lisa Bieser
Wizards of the Coast Team: David Gershman, Kate Irwin, Adam Lee, Hilary Ross, Liz Schuh
Illustrations: Conceptopolis, LLC

10 9 8 7

2020 Trade Paperback Boxed Set Edition

DUNGEONS & TOMBS

DUNGEONS & DRAGONS

DUNGEONS &
TOMBS

A Young Adventurer's Guide

WRITTEN BY JIM ZUB

WITH STACY KING AND ANDREW WHEELER

TEN SPEED PRESS
California | New York

CONTENTS

INTRODUCTION

Dungeons and tombs are places filled with adventure. Every door, a new mystery to be unearthed. Every encounter, a chance for victory or disaster.

This book is a tour through some of the most frightening and fatal places in the world of DUNGEONS & DRAGONS. It's a guide to their masters and myths, their creatures and corridors. It will show you six lethal lairs, introduce you to the beasts that live within, and then teach you how to construct your own diabolical dungeon.

Read this book from start to finish, or open it to any spot, get entranced by the cool artwork, and start your journey there. The more you read, the more you'll discover. The more you discover, the easier it will be to imagine your own heroic tales as you and your friends explore the unknown and gather hidden treasures.

Will your quest lead to fame, fortune, and songs sung of your deeds, or will your legend be lost in the shadow-filled crypts that have claimed countless other heroes? In the end, that's up to you. DUNGEONS & DRAGONS is all about unique adventures, and yours is about to begin.

Be brave!

PREPARING FOR YOUR DUNGEON DELVE

Before you head into the darkness, ready to explore and fight creatures fearsome and foul, you'll want to do a bit of preparation. Dungeon delving is a dangerous occupation. Adventurers with a bit of foresight and a plan tend to survive longer than those who charge empty-headedly into the unknown. Courage is good. Courage and the right tools for the job are even better. Think about these questions and then get ready for your journey.

- Who is in your adventuring party? Are you traveling alone or in a group? Check "Your Adventuring Party" on the facing page for some options, or build a more detailed set of characters using the *Warriors & Weapons* or *Wizards & Spells* books, which may also inform answers to the other questions.

- Where are you going? A cave, a castle, a swamp, a scorching desert, an undersea lair, a boneyard, or somewhere else? If the trek looks like it will be a long one, you'll want to make sure you bring bedrolls, blankets, a tent, and a way to light a fire. Are you prepared to hunt for food and forage for your meals, or are you bringing rations?

- What climate might you encounter once you get there? Hot or cold, bright or dark, wet or dry? Each possibility requires different clothing to stay comfortable. Can you see in the dark? If not, do you have a light source you can count on?

- Do you have a map of, or other knowledge about, the dungeon you seek? Any information at all is better than heading into a complete mystery. Legends, rumors, or local gossip may all prove helpful as you delve into fortresses, ruins, caverns, or crypts.

YOUR ADVENTURING PARTY

In DUNGEONS & DRAGONS, you and your friends take on the roles of adventurers who have banded together to fight monsters and gather treasure. Each hero will have their own special skills, determined by their character class. Here are a few of the most common types of heroes and their unique abilities.

- **Barbarian** Fierce, primal warriors capable of entering a mighty battle rage.

- **Bard** Magical entertainers who can inspire, heal, and create illusions through their performances.

- **Cleric** Faithful warriors who wield divine magic in service of a higher power.

- **Druid** Shapeshifting guardians who draw upon the power of nature.

- **Fighter** Soldiers and mercenaries trained in a variety of weapons and armor.

- **Monk** Masters of the martial arts who use mystic energy to empower their attacks.

- **Paladin** Holy champions who combine divine magic with martial skill.

- **Ranger** Scouts and trappers who blend fighting skills with keen knowledge of their surroundings to protect the wilderness.

- **Rogue** Thieves, acrobats, and explorers who specialize in stealth and trickery to overcome obstacles.

- **Sorcerer** Spellcasters whose power comes from their magical birthright.

- **Warlock** Magicians who gain their power through pacts with otherworldly creatures.

- **Wizard** Scholarly magic users who can manipulate reality itself.

THE MOST DANGEROUS DUNGEONS

Ahead lie six strange and sinister spaces ready to be uncovered by you and your fellow adventurers. Each dungeon profile covers the following important information:

OVERVIEW Background lore on the location, its purpose, and who currently controls it.

IMPORTANT PLACES Key regions within the dungeon that may help or hinder you on your journey.

SPOTLIGHT An in-depth look at a specific area in the dungeon so you can better understand the types of threats to be found, as well as story prompts to start you off on a thrilling quest.

ENCOUNTER A dramatic passage and a critical choice to help inspire your own tales of action and adventure.

IRONSLAG
A Giant's Fortress

In the icy mountains north of the Silver Marches sits Ironslag, the fortress home of fire giant Duke Zalto.

Ironslag is not only a fortress but also a massive forge, where iron ore mined from within the mountain was once smelted and turned into axes, war hammers, and other mighty weapons. Abandoned thousands of years ago, it has been restored and reopened by Zalto, who seeks to build a colossal war machine, the Vonindod, that will allow him to wage an epic war and rise through the ranks of the giant lords.

Anyone who dares venture into Ironslag will face treacherous yakfolk (the yikaria, see page 82), formidable salamanders, powerful fire giants, and the terrible duke himself—plus his equally dangerous family. This perilous quest must be undertaken to prevent Zalto from laying waste to the world—and to plunder the many treasures hidden deep in the mountain!

Are you prepared to risk your life and enter the fire giant's forge?

OVERVIEW

The caverns that form the forges and halls of Ironslag are concealed behind a five-hundred-foot-tall cliff face. Visitors must navigate their way past a village of treacherous yakfolk and through a labyrinth of mines before finally reaching the foundry and the personal quarters of Duke Zalto and his family.

IMPORTANT PLACES

The sprawling complex of Ironslag is most quickly entered through fifty-foot-tall doors that can only be opened by a fire giant's magical command. Since they're unlikely to open the doors to adventuring parties, you'll have to take the long way around, through the yikaria village and into the mines.

Yikaria Village: A small and seemingly idyllic settlement, but its fields and mill are operated by slaves. The yikaria are very welcoming, because every stranger is another potential captive.

The Mines: This confusing maze of tunnels is linked together by rail tracks for iron carts. Salamanders, fearsome half-humanoid, half-serpentine fire elementals that thrive in molten heat, keep an eye on the dwarfs and gnomes forced to work here.

The Foundry: Ogres on the upper section of the foundry tip iron ore from the carts into the smelters, while fire giants below keep the smelters burning so the ore can be melted down to make weapons. The foundry is unbearably hot.

Assembly Hall: The main hall of the fortress, where the parts of the Vonindod hang suspended by chains from a ninety-foot-tall ceiling, and where Duke Zalto himself often sits at his throne, attended by his fearsome giant hounds, Narthor and Zerebor.

Adamantine Forge: A forge so hot it can melt and mold adamantine weapons and armor. The energy required to power it is very rare, so it has lain dormant for thousands of years.

THE FOUNDRY

The foundry at Ironslag is where iron ore mined from the mountain is melted down to be turned into weapons. The overseer of the foundry is Duke Zalto's spoiled and lazy teenage son, Zaltember. When adventurers encounter Zaltember, the young fire giant may be threatening to toss a prisoner into the molten iron below, simply for his own amusement.

Heroic adventurers may wish to step in and save the prisoner from a toasty fate, which would guarantee a battle with Zaltember high on the gantries above the smelting pit. Even those adventurers less inclined to risk their lives for a stranger may realize that taking Zaltember hostage could be an advantage as they travel deeper into Ironslag and risk coming face-to-face with his powerful father.

Of course, starting a fight in a foundry is very dangerous! Zaltember is immune to fire, and you probably aren't. Those fire giants below can't reach you up here, can they?

STORY PROMPTS

Dungeon Master: Capturing Zaltember will give adventurers leverage against Duke Zalto, but as soon as the fight begins, the fire giants will hurl burning lumps of molten iron at the heroes.

Player Character: Think about what you could gain from confronting Zaltember and saving the prisoner—but also consider what you might risk! Have you assessed every threat in the room?

INTO THE FIRE

Erun held the wound in her side and gritted her teeth. She was in bad shape after battling with the orcs, and might not survive another fight. Yet what choice did she have? Everything they feared had come to pass. Duke Zalto now possessed an iron flask that contained a primordial power, an elemental goddess who could relight the adamantine forge. With it, he could reconstruct the Vonindod colossus and begin his rampage of terror.

Erun's companion, Braelle, gestured for her to stay still as Braelle drew her own frost blade. One of Zalto's giant hounds was sniffing around while the fire giant slept on his throne, the iron bottle lightly gripped in his hand. Either Erun or Braelle would have to steal it from him.

It was supposed to be Erun. She had performed a bardic rite that would prevent both Zalto and his dogs from detecting her. Yet she might still be caught, especially in her wounded state.

"Let me go in your place," whispered Braelle. "I can step into the shadows and appear at Zalto's side, vanishing again before he can react."

It seemed like a solid plan, except for one thing. Although Braelle was Erun's friend, she was also a warlock, forever bound to a lord of darkness. If Braelle stole the primordial power, would she be tempted to claim it for her dark master?

What should Erun do? If she tries to grab the flask herself, the attempt might cost her life. Is she strong enough to fight back if Duke Zalto awakens? On the other hand, if she trusts Braelle to do it, what will she do if her companion betrays her and tries to steal the flask? The choice is up to you!

THE TEMPLE OF ELEMENTAL EVIL

A Shrine of Darkness

A terrible threat gathers in the north. Monsters are on the prowl, and raiders target isolated homesteads. Sinister strangers whisper of fires and floods that will lay waste to this peaceful land.

Four rival cults have arisen, each with their own tactics but a shared mission: To serve a mysterious force called the Elder Elemental Eye and wipe out civilization. The cults use their chosen element—earth, air, fire, or water—to wreak havoc as they strive to bring their Prince of Elemental Evil through a dimensional portal into this world before the others can do the same.

The scattered towns of this frontier land face a dire threat. If the forces of Elemental Evil can't be defeated, madness and destruction will spread through Slumber Hills and, if left unchecked, perhaps the entire realm. Will you stand against the cultists, their Elemental Princes, and the ultimate power of the Elder Elemental Eye?

OVERVIEW

The Temple of Elemental Evil is a sprawling complex of towers and keeps built around an underground bastion that houses four separate temples, one each dedicated to earth, air, fire, and water. Below all of these is the Temple of the Elder Elemental Eye, a meeting point for the cultists and the center of Elemental Evil.

IMPORTANT PLACES

The quiet town of Red Larch provides an idyllic entry point to Slumber Hills, where the four cults have built their strongholds. An outer ring of aboveground structures surrounds the underground temples, allowing the cultists to keep watch and guard against intruders. Those who are able to fight their way past these outer defenses will find themselves in an underground fortress divided into four separate temples, one for each element.

Temple of Black Earth: Worshipping the implacable strength of elemental earth, the Cult of the Black Earth seeks to destroy civilizations with landslides, earthquakes, and sinkholes. They are the most defense-minded of the four cults, and their heavily guarded temple reflects this fact. They are led by a medusa named Marlos Urnrayle, who wields Ironfang, a war pick infused with the power of Ogrémoch, the Prince of Evil Earth.

Temple of Crushing Wave: The Cult of the Crushing Wave is devoted to the awesome power of water, building their temple around a large underground spring called the Dark Stream. Cultists use surging tides, flooding rivers, and the rock-crushing power of glaciers to defeat their enemies. Their prophet is Gar Shatterkeel, a former sailor who carries Drown, a trident imbued with the essence of Olhydra, the Princess of Evil Water.

Temple of Eternal Flame: The destructive power of fire in all its manifestations inspires the Cult of the Eternal Flame, who built their temple around an underground lava pool. Hot-tempered and violent, they want to burn away the civilized world with volcanic eruptions, forest fires, heat waves, and droughts. They are led by Vanifer, an ambitious tiefling who carries the dagger Tinderstrike, which is infused with the power of Imix, the Prince of Evil Fire.

Temple of Howling Hatred: Raging storms and violent winds have earned the devotion of the Cult of the Howling Hatred, whose temple is built around an enormous cavern that channels the forces of air to attack intruders. Illusionists and spies, these cultists prefer to strike from the shadows rather than engage in open battle. Aerisi Kalinoth, a willowy moon elf, is their prophet. She bears the spear Windvane, which channels the power of Yan-C-Bin, the Prince of Evil Air.

CAVERN OF THE LOST CROWN

As soon as anyone touches the crowned helmet within this former dwarven stronghold, the ghost of a treasure hunter named Reulek appears. He uses a horrifying magical scream to try and frighten away adventurers, warning, "Beware thieves! Even in death, the dwarves of Besilmer guard their fabled treasure!"

These words summon the spirits of four dwarven warriors, who attack all living creatures in the cavern. If you manage to defeat the ghosts, you can speak with Reulek, who was killed by the spirits in this cavern as he attempted to steal the crown.

Reulek's ghost believes he is now bound to the relic, trapping him for eternity. He asks you to help him by returning the lost crown to the tomb of the last king of Besilmer. In exchange, he can provide valuable information about the cultists, which will help in your quest.

STORY PROMPTS

Dungeon Master: Can Reulek be trusted, or will he betray the adventuring party? What happens if the party refuses to help?

Player Character: Is the information that Reulek offers worth the risk of helping him by returning the crown? What is the best choice in this situation—let him suffer the punishment for his theft, or help free his soul from this magic curse?

GARGOYLE GUARDIANS

After defeating the earth cultists at Sacred Stone Monastery, Redclay and her companion, the wizard Inowyn, tracked the fleeing survivors to this vast chasm. Somewhere beyond the stone bridge, Marlos Urnrayle, the Prophet of Evil Earth, carried out his destructive plans.

"I'll take the one on the bridge," Redclay said, pointing her sword toward the two gargoyles who guarded the trestle. "You focus on the flyer."

As Redclay prepared to attack, Inowyn whispered a quick warning. "Wait! Do you see it? There, in the shadows?"

Redclay followed the half-elf's gesture toward the distant rocks, where she spotted the faint, craggy outline of a third gargoyle. While she was grateful for Inowyn's keen perception, she also realized their chances of success were now much worse.

"We still have those cultist robes we found at Sacred Stone," Inowyn said. "Maybe we should try sneaking past them?"

Redclay considered the options and frowned. A fight at the entrance would draw attention that they didn't want, and perhaps even give Marlos a chance to flee. On the other hand, if they tried to infiltrate by pretending to be cultists and failed, they'd lose the element of surprise and almost certainly be captured, making their quest even more difficult.

Should Redclay and Inowyn attempt a surprise attack on the gargoyles, risking their whole mission if the battle is noisy enough to alert the Temple to their presence? Would they be better off trying to sneak their way inside disguised as cultists—and what happens if their ruse fails? The choice is yours!

THE SEA GHOST

A Pirate Ship

The *Sea Ghost* is not a famous ship. You won't have heard of it, you wouldn't recognize it, and, if you're lucky, you'll never encounter it. As its name suggests, this "ghost" means to pass quietly through the night and leave little trace behind. If you *do* see this specter, you might be marked next for the grave.

The *Sea Ghost* is a smuggling ship crewed by pirates, though it also keeps a few secrets beneath its decks and among the barrels and crates of stolen goods and contraband.

The captain is a mean-spirited swashbuckler by the name of Sigurd Snake Eyes, and he's been using the *Sea Ghost* to smuggle goods in and out of the sleepy town of Saltmarsh for years.

The good people of Saltmarsh have had enough of this criminal tricking their town and stealing their treasure. Someone needs to board the *Sea Ghost* under cover of night and put an end to these pirates and their wicked ways.

OVERVIEW

The *Sea Ghost* is a single-sail ship, ninety feet long from prow to stern and twenty-six feet across at its widest point. Its main deck sits about nine feet above the waterline, with cabins at fore and aft. The ship is made largely of wood, though every part is slick with saltwater.

IMPORTANT PLACES

To board the *Sea Ghost*, you first must wait for it to come to you. That means setting up a watch on the shores of Saltmarsh until the smuggling ship makes its next visit and then rowing out to meet it. Adventurers face a choice between sneaking aboard from the seaward side of the ship while the crew is busy signaling the shore, or bluffing the smugglers into lowering a rope ladder.

Decks: If the alarm is raised upon boarding the *Sea Ghost*, adventurers will likely face an all-out battle on the slippery decks of the ship. Mind your feet!

Cabins and Galley: Beneath the raised forecastle and poop deck at the fore and aft of the ship are some of the ship's most important rooms, including the captain's cabin, the galley, and a cabin where some unexpected guests are staying—a trio of fierce and terrible lizardfolk, reptilian humanoids who prefer to settle in marshy swamps.

Cargo Hold: Below the main deck are the crew's quarters and the cargo hold. The hold contains most of the contraband that the ship is smuggling, though some rare treasures may lurk elsewhere on board.

The Bilge: You never know where smugglers might stash their treasure. Maybe even in the space between the lower deck and the hull? Or maybe the only things lurking down here are flesh-burrowing rot grubs?

Crow's Nest: Forty feet above the deck and accessible only by rope ladder is a lookout point at the top of the ship's mast. Adventurers who lack caution may get a nasty surprise when one of the smugglers starts raining arrows down on their heads!

THE MAIN DECK

The main deck of the *Sea Ghost* presents the most obvious opportunity for an open battle between adventurers and pirates. There's a wide slippery wooden floor, ropes from which to swing, and barrels to hurl, and it provides you with the chance to toss people overboard! It's the perfect place for a swashbuckling sword fight, and perhaps the only place on the ship where long-distance attacks will be effective.

However, there are also several cabins that open directly onto the deck, and adventurers don't know what lurks behind those doors. There may be vast treasures—or reinforcements.

Will your adventure aboard the *Sea Ghost* involve sneaking stealthily from room to room, or will it be an all-out brawl beneath the moonlight?

STORY PROMPTS

Dungeon Master: You know who is on this ship, but your adventurers do not. When is the best time to surprise them with an attack by lizardfolk?

Player Character: What's the best way to deal with the enemies in front of you before someone raises the alarm and brings other foes to the deck?

THE SECRET IN THE WALLS

Avaron figured it would be easy enough. While his fellow adventurers fought the pirates on the deck above, he would sneak below and pick through the cabins for the best treasures the *Sea Ghost* had to offer.

No one would have ever known, if he hadn't bumped a chair in the darkness. The noise brought the ship's conjurer to investigate, and Avaron was forced to retreat into the nearest empty cabin—only it wasn't empty after all.

Following the scratching noises from behind the wall, Avaron quickly found a secret panel leading to a hidden cell. Inside was a young sea elf blinking against the dim light, with chains binding his wrists and ankles.

Whoever this sea elf was, he was no friend of the pirates. Avaron could pick the elf's locks easily, maybe gaining an ally against the pirates when they tried to escape. Although looking at the state of him, the elf would probably need Avaron's last healing potion before he'd be any use in a fight.

Should Avaron trust the captured elf and hope they can battle the pirates together? Or would he have a better chance on his own? What will Avaron do if the elf turns out to be secretly in league with the pirates—or part of a plan to help the lizardfolk take over the ship, ruining Avaron's plans to make off with the pirate's stolen treasure? It's up to you to decide!

RAVENLOFT
A Vampire's Castle

In Barovia, a place of perpetual night, stands a terrifying castle that protects and imprisons the lord of this land. The citadel is called Ravenloft, and its owner is a powerful magic-wielding vampire named Strahd Von Zarovich.

Ravenloft is an opulent old castle adorned with gothic finery. It's protected by undead creatures, including skeletons, ghosts, werewolves, and, of course, vampire spawn. Its halls are dim and filled with all manners of curses and traps to ensnare any who dare trespass upon the count's property. Beneath the stronghold are burial chambers and prisons littered with old relics and deranged unliving monstrosities.

For as long as Count Strahd has been cursed with undead might, the sun has not risen in Barovia, and it will stay that way until a group of heroes finds the courage within themselves to fight back against the darkness and stop his reign of terror.

Do you dare venture into Ravenloft's frightening halls and twisting crypts?

OVERVIEW

Castle Ravenloft is a massive stone-built structure filled with secrets and danger. Its highest tower stands three hundred sixty feet tall, looming over the Barovian countryside, a constant reminder of Strahd's incredible power and influence.

IMPORTANT PLACES

Castle Ravenloft is surrounded by fifty-foot-wide chasms on all sides that plummet into eerie fog below. The drawbridge, normally closed unless the count is expecting visitors, is the only safe non-magical way across. Strahd leaves his gates and doors unlocked, confident that anyone foolish enough to enter will either be destroyed by his many minions, or, in rare cases, survive long enough to earn his personal attention.

Dining Hall: A massive chamber lit by three magnificent crystal chandeliers. A long, heavy table covered with fine satin cloth sits at the center of this room and a floor-to-ceiling pipe organ stands against the far wall.

Chapel: Once a holy place, the chapel was spoiled and left in disarray by Strahd's curse.

The Heart of Sorrow: A ten-foot-diameter glowing red crystal floating within one of the castle towers. This strange, magical formation absorbs pain inflicted on its vampiric master, an added level of protection that Strahd uses to survive against any foe foolish enough to attack him.

Hall of Heroes: A room of ten stone statues depicting Strahd's ancestors. Their spirits may provide important answers about the vampire's past and his weaknesses.

Catacombs: Forty crypts, some simple and unmarked, others ornate and covered with carvings and dedications, are organized in rows beneath the castle. Each one may contain a corpse, a creature, or hidden treasures.

Strahd's Tomb: Only the bravest and most well-prepared adventurers will be able to find Strahd's resting place and fight him in his own domain. Failure means death and then returning to life as one of the count's many vampiric servants.

THE BRAZIER ROOM

Beneath Castle Ravenloft, you'll find many different vaults—crypts, prisons, an armory, and a torture chamber. Among them is a strange room that provides a magical shortcut to any destination—or to a deadly demise for those who disturb its furnishings.

A stone brazier burns in the center of the room, but its tall white flame produces no heat. Around it are seven spheres made of tinted glass, each a different color. Above it hangs a large wood-framed hourglass, with glowing text written around the base.

> Cast a stone into the fire: Violet leads to the mountain spire
> Orange to the castle's peak / Red if lore is what you seek
> Green to where the coffins hide / Indigo to the master's bride
> Blue to ancient magic's womb / Yellow to the master's tomb

If you cast a colored sphere into the white flame, the fire changes hue to match and the hourglass's sand begins to drain. Touching the colored flame doesn't burn; instead, it magically transports you to a different part of the castle or elsewhere within the land of Barovia. After thirty seconds, the sand runs out, the fire changes back to white, and the glass sphere reappears, resetting the magic to be used again.

Two enchanted iron golems guard this space. If triggered, they attack all intruders with poison gas and crushing blows from their hooves and armor.

STORY PROMPTS

Dungeon Master: What brings the iron golems to life and makes them attack? Where will the brazier send your adventuring party—somewhere safe, or into greater danger?

Player Character: Will you use the power of the white flame to transport yourself to somewhere unknown?

SHOWDOWN WITH COUNT STRAHD

Ezmerelda averted her eyes and gasped as magic fire engulfed the hallway in an explosion of heat that seared her lungs. Almost as soon as the fire erupted, it stopped; Victor collapsed in pain, his battered plate armor smoking and charred.

Strahd chuckled as the last wisps of flame rippled from his hand. "All who oppose the Master of Ravenloft learn their place. You should feel honored that I chose to dispose of you personally instead of leaving it to my faithful followers."

Ezmerelda held aloft her silver-plated shortsword and prepared to attack Strahd again. She could tell for all the count's bravado, the vampire was wounded and the potent spell had used up his strength. This could be her chance to finally end the vampire's reign of terror upon the people of Barovia.

Strahd sensed her resolve and was in no rush to test his might against hers. Before Ezmerelda could strike, the master vampire began turning to mist. As his features shimmered and diffused, he cackled, "You know where my crypt lies, foolish child. Follow me there and battle to your last breath, or save your friend and live to fight another day. . . ."

Should Ezmerelda stay with Victor and carry him to safety, saving his life? Or should she follow Strahd back to his coffin, taking this rare chance to strike while the count is injured—an opportunity that might not come again? It's up to you!

CHULT

An Island of Dinosaurs

Chult is a wild and beautiful island where blue waves lap against golden beaches, and wide rivers wend lazily through lush, green forests. On first glimpse, it may seem like a paradise. But you won't have to travel far into its verdant interior to have that illusion shattered.

The island is a dangerous and deadly place where almost everything seems designed to kill you, from carnivorous plants to militant frogs, hidden pit traps to angry gods. Chult's most notorious inhabitants include people-eating dinosaurs, brain-devouring zombies, and an undead spellcaster named Acererak. (And those are just the threats that have been reported!) Much of the island remains unexplored by outsiders—or, more accurately, many explorers have ventured forth and never come back.

Even still, Chult is a land of treasure where rich civilizations have risen and fallen, and artifacts of great power have disappeared. Merchants from around the world have tried to exploit the island's natural wealth but failed. For many who delve deep into the tropics of Chult, it is a paradise. For others, it is their tomb.

OVERVIEW

Chult is a vast tropical island that calls to explorers, many of
whom long to conquer its untamed forests and discover its secrets.
Largely cut off from the world by the formidable mountains that
line its coast, Chult harbors many mysteries, and has infinite ways
to keep them hidden.

IMPORTANT PLACES

To reach Chult, you'll need to sail the Sea of Broken Dreams and land at Port Nyanzaru, the island's only modern city. You can get information and supplies from local merchants—and get your pocket picked by the local thieves' guild, if you're not careful. From Port Nyanzaru, you can explore the island's many forts, mines, and temples, and what remains of the civilizations that once thrived here.

Hrakhamar: A dwarven forge that was abandoned after being flooded by volcanic magma. Firenewts have since taken over the caverns. The magma has receded, and now dwarves want to reclaim it.

Jahaka Anchorage: A sea cave so large that ships can find safe shelter within its walls. The cave offers easy access to the jungle, but the merchants that use it are not always welcoming to strangers. (Rumor has it they're not entirely legitimate traders.)

Nangalore: Ornate and palatial terraced gardens that long ago fell into disrepair, though the queen they were built to honor is said to still lurk among the ruins, transformed by grief and dark magic into something terrible!

Omu: Chult's great lost city, once known for its wealth and splendor, has been reclaimed by the jungle. Twisted vines have consumed its famous shrines, and dinosaurs roam its streets.

Fane of the Night Serpent: The yuan-ti, a tribe of devious snakepeople, are the dominant force in fallen Omu. They reside in this expansive temple beneath the city's former palace.

Tomb of the Nine Gods: Omu was once ruled by nine trickster gods, who were destroyed many centuries ago. In their place has risen the archlich Acererak, who transforms the souls of fallen heroes into fuel for his evil magic.

DUNGRUNGLUNG

If your travels through the jungles of Chult bring you to Dungrunglung, a settlement of the aggressive and territorial froglike grungs, you may find yourself entangled in a very strange adventure. The vain and short-tempered grung king, Groak, wants to conduct a ritual to summon the goddess Nangnang to be his bride. The high priestess, Krr'ook, fears for her life if the ceremony fails, and she believes that outsiders may be able to help her fool the king.

Grungs may not look like much, but their numbers, agility, and sheer ferocity make them dangerous, and you're unlikely to pass through their territory without getting in trouble. You can distract and flatter King Groak for a time, but your best hope of surviving an encounter with the grungs may be to make an alliance with Krr'ook to aid in her schemes.

STORY PROMPTS

Dungeon Master: How can you place your adventurers at Groak's mercy, so that an alliance with Krr'ook is their only way out?

Player Character: How would you fool a mad king into believing that his goddess has manifested in front of him?

THE SCHEMES OF RAS NSI

In service to his merciful goddess, young half-orc Kez ventured into the fallen city of Omu, hoping to end the terror of Ras Nsi, a fellow paladin corrupted by a dark god and returned from death as a serpentine necromancer. He had heard tell of such abominations, deathless beasts summoned back to life in decay and wickedness, and expected a brutal fight.

He did not expect a monkey. A vicious little screeching, flying monkey that tore at him with its tiny hands and feet.

Kez tried to ignore the little beast as he reached for his sacred medallion—a gift from his goddess—which he believed could send Ras Nsi to oblivion. It contained a spell for destroying the undead, one powerful enough to vanquish even this villain.

But then, the medallion was gone. Kez panicked as the monkey flew down the dank corridor with the amulet gripped in its paws.

Kez had sworn an oath that he would end Ras Nsi's reign of terror this night. Now fear and doubt crept into his soul. Could he accomplish his destiny without his goddess's blessing?

Should Kez chase after his stolen medallion, knowing that Ras Nsi might escape—and how will he get it back from the tricky flying monkey if he chooses this path? Or should he confront Ras Nsi directly, hoping to prevail even without his powerful holy weapon? The choice is yours!

UNDERMOUNTAIN

Grand Dungeon of the Mad Mage

Undermountain is the largest, deepest dungeon of them all. Burrowing through and under Mount Waterdeep are miles upon miles of tunnels, ranging from wide, well-carved passageways to narrow cracks roughly cut from raw rock.

All this is the work of the Mad Mage, Halaster Blackcloak, a wizard who has spent the last thousand years building this massive and dangerous dungeon. He has stocked it with terrifying creatures from across the lands, ensuring his privacy as he continues his eccentric eldritch experiments deep underground.

Treasure and glory await any adventurers brave enough to enter the sprawling labyrinth of Undermountain, but so do mighty monsters, terrifying traps, and the risk of madness. Something strange and rotten lies at the heart of Undermountain, a mysterious force that twists the minds of all who approach.

Are you ready to risk your sanity to plunder the rewards that await below?

OVERVIEW

Undermountain is a complex dungeon containing hundreds of miles of passageways and rooms, all buried beneath enormous Mount Waterdeep. At its core resides the Mad Mage, a powerful wizard obsessed with expanding both his dungeon and his magical knowledge.

IMPORTANT PLACES

The only access point to Undermountain is through the Yawning Portal, a warm and friendly inn built above the ruins of the Mad Mage's original wizard tower. Once inside, explorers will face a seemingly endless maze of hallways and rooms, each layer built in a different style and harboring its own unique dangers.

Arcane Chambers: The ruins of the Mad Mage's original dwelling, this area has been overtaken by goblins who run a market for denizens of Undermountain. It is a huge hall with sixty-foot-high ceilings supported by two rows of stone pillars.

Caverns of Ooze: A series of naturally formed tunnels and chambers carved out by the slow passage of primordial slime. This is the dwelling place for a huge gray ooze and two intelligent black puddings, among other nasty creatures.

Crystal Labyrinth: This glittering area is carved from multihued crystal and features several large caverns with soaring ceilings studded with sparkling stalactites.

Slitherswamp: Muck-filled caverns and damp, dangerous shrubbery make up this watery level, which is filled with humidity, buzzing insects, and the remains of an evil serpent cult.

Trobriand's Graveyard: Known as the Metal Mage, Trobriand specialized in creating magical constructs from steel and iron. Eventually he transferred his own consciousness into one of his bizarre creations. This area is filled with metallic monstrosities and voracious rust monsters.

The Mad Mage's Lair: The residence of Halaster Blackcloak, this area features an upside-down library, a room filled with talking heads in jars, an animated hallway that never stops moving, and a portal that leads to Halaster's Tower, a three-story spire that crosses over into another dimension.

THE DRAGON'S HATCHERY

Undermountain is home to a dizzying array of creatures, but even among this menagerie, the red dragon Ashtyrranthor and her six children make an impression. The dragon family resides in a series of majestic tunnels beneath the Crystal Labyrinth, heated by lava pools and protected by magical illusions.

The highlight of these chambers is a hatchery, where a dragon egg rests gently in the center of the lava pool. Many a magical scholar would pay handsomely for such a treasure, leaving your party with quite a dilemma. You could try to steal the egg, either for your own magical research or to sell to a wealthy patron. You could destroy it, preventing the birth of a dangerous dragon. Or you could leave it be, knowing that dragons are fiercely protective of their offspring.

Whatever you decide, you'll have to do it quickly—within this part of the dragon's lair, the temperature, at 120 degrees Fahrenheit, is too high for non-dragons to handle for more than an hour. Make sure your party comes to a decision quietly as well. Loud noises in the hatchery will surely draw the attention of Ashtyrranthor!

STORY PROMPTS

Dungeon Master: Is the dragon egg real, or only a clever fake like the other illusion rooms in the lair?

Player Character: Will you risk stealing the dragon egg, or continue exploring in hopes of finding better treasure? If you try to reach the egg, what techniques can you use to avoid scorching yourself on the lava?

BLACKCLOAK'S BARGAIN

Urnath grunted as another of the metallic insects crunched beneath her war hammer. Before she could savor the victory, her companion, Puknik, shouted a warning, directing her attention toward the ceiling. Moments ago there had only been twisted metal and the angry buzz of the mechanical wasps, but now a grinning man in elegant wizard robes hovered in the same spot.

"The Mad Mage!" cried Puknik, before unleashing a *magic missile* spell. The glowing arrows passed harmlessly through the illusion. "Though not in the flesh. . . ."

"Of course not, you foolish spell-slinger," replied Halaster Blackcloak with a giggle. "I have a task for you. A trifle, really. Clear out these metal creations, leftovers from my former apprentice, Trobriand, and I'll reward you handsomely. A magical hammer for you, and a scroll containing one of my custom spells for your friend. What say you?"

The companions traded a solemn glance. Who knew how many of these creatures there were, and how much time it would take from their real quest, rescuing a kidnapped nobleman from his goblin captors. But, if they failed to accept this new task, the Mad Mage's anger would likely turn against them, making their original mission even more difficult, if not impossible. Unable to speak freely in front of Blackcloak, Urnath and Puknik must decide quickly.

Should they accept this new quest, or continue on their original mission? What are the odds that Blackcloak will keep his promise if they succeed? Or will the Mad Mage change his mind and betray them at a crucial moment? Is there a way to accomplish both quests in the limited time available? Where the story goes is up to you!

DUNGEON BESTIARY

Dungeons are fascinating and fearsome, filled with danger and despair, traps and treasures. Some are abandoned strongholds from ancient times, while others are natural caves or lairs carved out by foul beasts. Most have been in use for centuries, building up layers of enchantment and distinctive features that give birth to entirely new types of monsters.

The hidden nooks of a dungeon are fertile breeding ground for all manner of fungi, vermin, and scavengers. Once-normal beasts are sometimes warped by living underground for generations, evolving in unusual and deadly ways. Spellcasters create magical servants and powerful guardians who persist in their tasks long after their creator has moved on or passed away.

Designed to thrive in harsh and violent environments, these creatures are ruthless and lethal. Whatever form they take, beasts bred for dungeon life are among the deadliest a hero will ever face.

DANGER LEVELS

Each monster profile includes a number indicating the danger level of that creature, with a **0** being harmless, a **1** as a reasonable threat for a beginning adventurer, and building up from there. A **5** is incredibly dangerous and requires an experienced group of adventurers to possibly defeat it. There are some **epic** creatures more powerful than a mere number can define. Such terrors can only be fought by legendary heroes armed with the most powerful magic weapons and spells imaginable.

BASILISK

TRAINING A BASILISK Basilisk eggs are a rare treasure because a basilisk raised from an egg can be trained to obey its master! As you might imagine, basilisks make excellent—if nasty—"guard dogs."

SIZE Basilisks are large reptilian creatures with bodies that grow to about six feet in length, and tails that can grow just as long, making them, overall, about the size of a large Komodo dragon.

Basilisks are terrifying predators due to the unique way they snare their prey. Their cold gaze has the power of petrification, which means they can turn flesh to stone. Once their prey is transformed, a basilisk can crush the resulting statue in its formidable jaws, with the stone turning back into meat as the basilisk swallows. It's a terrible way to meet your fate!

Encountering a basilisk does not mean instant death. If you're tough enough, you might survive the initial glance. However, the moment the effect takes hold, only the right spell or an antidote can save you.

Some alchemists can make basilisk antidote from the creature's guts; but to do that, you need to hunt a basilisk—and you don't want to hunt a basilisk without the antidote handy, so you can see the conundrum.

LAIR Basilisks prefer sheltered lairs in warm climates, such as caves in a dry rocky desert or a burrow in a tropical forest. One easy way to tell if a basilisk has made a home nearby is to look for the remains of its prey in the form of shattered statues.

DO THIS

Polish your shield or sword. A reflective metal surface can sometimes trick a basilisk into attacking itself.

Run! Basilisks are not very fast, because they don't need to be.

DON'T DO THIS

Don't look directly at a basilisk. It needs only one glance to start turning you to stone.

Don't ignore statues. Ruined statues can indicate a nearby basilisk—especially statues of unusual subjects, standing in strange poses or looking afraid.

FLAMESKULL

2

SPECIAL POWERS

SPELLCASTING
Flameskulls retain some magical powers, and can cast some lower-level spells such as *magic missile*, *shield*, *flaming sphere*, and *fireball*.

REJUVENATION
When destroyed, a flameskull can reassemble itself to full health within one hour, unless holy water is sprinkled on the remains to dispel its magic.

SIZE A flameskull is the size of a normal skull for the humanoid from which it was created, except surrounded by a half-foot of crackling flames.

These magical guardians can only be created from the skulls of dead wizards, and make excellent protectors for a spellcaster's secrets. Perpetually burning with bright-green flame, flameskulls drift and cackle through their assigned patrols, having been driven mad by the ritual that made them.

Flameskulls will attack intruders on sight, spitting fire rays from their mouths. Flameskulls can also cast a spell called *mage hand*, which lets them open doors and move small objects even though they no longer have hands of their own. Halaster Blackcloak, the Mad Mage of Undermountain, has a number of flameskulls that he uses to guard his secrets and spy on those who enter his dungeon.

LAIR Most flameskulls will be found within the lairs of their creators, powerful spellcasters who may reside in a wizard tower, an underground dungeon, or a vast ancient library. They may also be found within the ruins where a spellcaster once lived, carrying out their ghostly routines.

DO THIS

Disperse your party. You'll be harder for a flameskull to hit with a fireball if you split up, instead of bunching together.

Splash a dead flameskull with holy water. Otherwise, the creature will come back to life in one hour.

DON'T DO THIS

Don't rely on magic to win. Flameskulls have magic resistance, so it's easier to defeat one with physical weapons.

Don't try to reason with it. Flameskulls remember almost nothing from their former lives, except for the magic spells that they can still cast.

GIBBERING MOUTHER

SPECIAL POWERS

BLINDING SPITTLE
The mouther spits a chemical glob up to fifteen feet, which explodes on impact to release a bright flash that temporarily blinds all creatures within a five-foot radius.

GIBBERING
The manic babbling of a gibbering mouther can paralyze a target with fear, making them unable to escape as the creature moves closer. This effect impacts all adventurers within twenty feet.

SIZE A gibbering mouther is about the height of a professional basketball player and as wide at the bottom as a dining room table. Their elastic flesh does not have a fixed shape, but instead stretches and squishes as the creature moves.

Of all the monsters animated by evil sorcery, the gibbering mouther may be the most nightmarish. These foul creatures are covered with the eyes, mouths, and melting flesh of their former victims. They shamble and ooze through dungeons in search of their next prey, driven mad by the wicked magic that animates them. The very ground dissolves around them as they move, creating a mudlike surface that is difficult to escape.

Endlessly hungry, gibbering mouthers cannot contain their excitement if they sense prey is nearby. Their multiple mouths begin to mumble and chatter, each with its own unique voice. This cacophony can drive anyone who hears it temporarily mad. Some may flee in panic, while others are transfixed to the spot, unable to move as the gibbering mouther slowly flows over them and begins dissolving their flesh.

LAIR Gibbering mouthers are created by evil magic and often found in the dungeons of powerful, villainous spellcasters. They move slowly across solid ground but can swim easily through water, quicksand, and mud, making them adaptable to a variety of dungeon environments.

DO THIS

Cover your ears. If you can't hear the gibbering mouther, it can't leave you frozen in fear.

Rescue your pals. Even if a party member is enveloped by a gibbering mouther, you still have a chance to rescue them—at least, until you see a pair of familiar eyes pop up on the creature's body!

DON'T DO THIS

Don't get too close. The ground around a gibbering mouther is uneven and perilous. Distance attacks are your safest bet.

Don't ignore its teeth. The noises from all those mouths can be dangerous, but don't forget that numerous mouths also means many, many sharp teeth.

GRUNG

SPECIAL POWERS

STANDING LEAP
From a standing position, grungs can instantly leap up to fifteen feet in the air or twenty-five feet ahead of their former positions, allowing them to quickly strike opponents during combat.

POISON EXCRETION
All grungs excrete a dangerous poison that is harmless to them but nasty to any other type of creature.

SIZE Even the tallest grung is too short to reach the countertop in a human kitchen (maybe that's why they're so grumpy!). They have stocky bodies with thin legs, but their sticky toepads give them excellent balance.

Grungs are small, and to some they may appear cute, but they're certainly not harmless. These brightly colored froglike humanoids should never be underestimated. In fact, they can hurt you without even trying, thanks to the poisonous residue that seeps naturally from their skin. Just touching a Grung is enough to do serious damage!

Grungs are also dangerous because they're belligerent, bad-tempered, and more than happy to cause trouble. They're proudly defensive of their territory and can leap up to twenty-five feet in a single bound, appearing as if out of nowhere with their weapons drawn once they land. Some grungs can also make a sound that briefly stuns or mesmerizes their foes.

Grungs live in a strictly divided society, with each grung taking on the color of their assigned social role as they grow older. Green grungs are fighters and workers, blue grungs are artisans and homemakers, purple grungs are administrators, red grungs are scholars, orange grungs are elite warriors, and gold grungs are the ruling class.

LAIR Most grungs live on the Isle of Chult, making their homes in the festering swamps. They need to be close to water at all times, and prefer shady locations with lots of plant cover.

DO THIS

Stay dry. Grungs prefer wet terrain, but all that dampness will have a negative effect on your weapons and other gear.

Offer to help. Grungs want to protect their territory. If you can demonstrate you're not a threat, and offer to help them against someone who is, they might listen.

DON'T DO THIS

Don't touch. The poison on grung skin can take effect in an instant.

Don't be fooled by their size. Grungs may look tiny, but they pack a punch that hits harder than you'd expect.

IRON GOLEM

4

SPECIAL POWERS

FIRE ABSORPTION
Created in the blazing heat of a forge, iron golems are not only immune to fire damage, they can actually heal when attacked by flames!

POISONOUS BREATH
Iron golems exhale a fifteen-foot cone of poison gas, which damages anyone exposed to the noxious fumes.

SIZE Iron golems can be created in any size, from eight to sixteen feet tall, depending on how much raw material their creator has on hand. Most range in height from the top of a volleyball net to the bottom of a basketball hoop.

An iron golem is a living statue made of heavy metal. Every step it takes shakes the ground beneath its feet and its fists hit like giant hammers, crushing whatever gets in the way.

Golems are created using powerful magic, binding a spirit to an inanimate object. Iron golems are the most powerful, as their bodies are nearly impervious to harm. They can spout deadly poison gas and smash almost anything standing in their way. These unstoppable juggernauts exist only to do the bidding of their creators, protecting and attacking mindlessly as ordered.

LAIR As constructs who must obey all orders they are given, golems do not have a natural lair. They can often be found guarding the residence or workshop of the spellcaster who created them. Since they do not age, iron golems can be found in abandoned ruins, still obeying the orders of a creator who has long since died and gone to dust.

DO THIS

Break out the magic. Regular weapons won't even scratch an iron golem. You'll need magic to get through their iron shell.

Stay clear of poison gas. Once you see the golem start to spew its cloud of deadly smoke, move back and try to attack it from behind.

DON'T DO THIS

Don't get underfoot. If you get too close, an iron golem can smash you beneath its huge stomping feet.

Don't use fire. Heating the metal of an iron golem heals the creature instead of hurting it.

LIZARDFOLK

1

SPECIAL POWERS

MULTI-ATTACK
Highly trained warriors, lizardfolk can make two attacks each round, choosing between their sharp bites, heavy clubs, thrown javelins, and spiked shields to damage their enemies.

BREATH HOLDING
Lizardfolk can go without breathing for up to 15 minutes, enabling them to fight underwater and resist attack by poison gas.

SIZE Lizardfolk are slightly taller than humans, with broad torsos and thick tails that give them extra bulk. Imagine a bodybuilder with a huge reptile tail and you're on the right track.

Lizardfolk are a race of reptilian humanoids who generally keep to their own society, living in simple tribal communes usually led by a sole chieftain. They prefer to settle in areas of marsh and swamp, and they often build their homes in dank caves, from which they set out on their daily hunts.

Though lizardfolk can eat almost anything, they have a strong preference for meat, and by some reports they especially enjoy human flesh. Anyone venturing into lizardfolk territory could find themselves marked as prey.

Larger than humans, and with tough scaly hides, lizardfolk are intimidating creatures, and unwary travelers should make note of their snapping teeth and razor-sharp claws. Though lizardfolk hunt and fight with weapons, they're still very dangerous when unarmed!

LAIR Lizardfolk can be found in swamps and jungles, where they stake out hunting grounds with camouflaged scouts who keep watch for any intruders. These fiercely territorial creatures do not appreciate visitors, although they may throw a feast to celebrate your arrival—you'll be the main dish, however.

DO THIS	DON'T DO THIS
Watch the teeth. Don't be so distracted by a lizardfolk's weapon attack that you don't notice them lunging for a bite of your tantalizing flesh!	**Don't get in their way.** Lizardfolk are great hunters; if they're tracking prey, you don't want to give them a reason to switch focus!
Stay stealthy. If you must cross through lizardfolk territory, do so quietly and carefully if you want to avoid a tough fight.	**Don't assume they're simple.** Tribal communities often do things in ways that others are not used to, but that doesn't mean they're unsophisticated. Every community has its own systems and culture.

MIMIC

☠ 1

SPECIAL POWERS

SHAPECHANGE

Mimics can hide their true forms, appearing instead as a wide range of inanimate objects. This deception can't be detected so long as the mimic remains motionless. When killed, the creature reverts back to its true form.

ADHESION

Mimics give off a gooey substance that sticks both creatures and objects to its body. Any limb or weapon stuck to the creature can't be used to fight it, so you'll need to get unstuck quickly if you want to survive!

SIZE Disguised, mimics are the average size of the object they are imitating, so about two feet tall for a chest to six feet tall for a door. They rarely shift entirely into their natural form, but when they do, they appear as a lumpy blob between three and five feet tall.

Not everything in a dungeon is what it appears to be. Mimics are shapeshifting predators that take the form of inanimate objects to lure in their prey (hint: that's you). In dungeons, mimics most often appear as doors or treasure chests, although they can take on many different shapes.

They can alter their appearance to look like wood, metal, stone, and other basic materials, making them indistinguishable from the original object they are copying. Once their prey gets close enough, the monsters spout pseudopods and attack. Mimics excrete a sticky substance when they change shape, which helps them hang on to both victims and the victims' weapons.

LAIR Mimics live and hunt alone, seeking out well-traveled spots within dungeons where they can be assured of a steady stream of prey. They sometimes share their lairs with other creatures, although their predatory instincts make them bad roommates.

DO THIS

Approach with caution. Don't let your excitement of possible treasure blind you to the risk that a tempting chest may represent.

Poke it with a stick. Using a quarterstaff or walking stick to prod at inanimate objects before touching them can help you avoid a mimic.

DON'T DO THIS

Don't focus on melee attacks. The sticky surfaces of mimics mean that swords and other melee weapons can become trapped on their skin, making it impossible to keep fighting. Try a ranged attack instead!

OOZE

SIZE Oozes range in size from five to fifteen square feet. Gray oozes tend to be smallest, while gelatinous cubes are often large enough to fill an average dungeon hallway.

Black Pudding

Gelatinous Cube

Gray Ooze

Ochre Jelly

Human

Oozes dwell in the darkness. These slimy creatures slither through dungeons in search of prey, swallowing up everything they find, before slowly dissolving it within their shambling forms. Drawn to movement and warmth, they are constantly seeking fresh victims. Death by ooze is deeply unpleasant, as it often takes several hours for the creature to gradually melt its victim's flesh. On the plus side, this slow dissolution can give a target the time needed to be rescued by their allies.

Oozes have no sense of tactics or self-preservation. They behave in predictable ways, moving toward possible prey and away from bright lights. Because oozes are not intelligent, smarter creatures can manipulate them into serving as unwitting allies, guarding important passageways or serving as traps for unwary adventurers. Since oozes' corrosive effects do not work on most metal, jewels, and magical items, an ooze's corpse can be a rich source of treasure for victorious adventurers.

LAIR Oozes are capable of making a home in any dark, dank dungeon space. They cluster in gloomy corners where they can slowly dissolve their victims without being disturbed, but can also be found shambling through busy (but unlit) hallways in search of fresh food.

DO THIS

Light your way. Oozes are sensitive to bright lights and will move away from dungeon areas that are highly illuminated.

Beware of clean floors. Most dungeons don't have maid service. If the ground is swept clean of all debris, the odds are good that an ooze has passed by recently.

DON'T DO THIS

Don't give up on a swallowed ally. Oozes take hours to fully digest their prey. Even if a party member is swallowed by one, you may still have time to rescue them.

Don't wait for nap time. These unnatural creatures don't require sleep, so it's hard to catch them off guard.

BLACK PUDDING

2

A black pudding appears as a heaving mass of sticky black sludge. It prefers dark passageways, where it can blend in with the shadows. Experienced adventurers know that a clean hallway is a warning that a black pudding has swept through recently.

SPECIAL POWERS

CORROSION
Black pudding dissolves flesh, wood, metal, and bone. Touching it with bare skin burns like acid, and non-magical weapons are damaged by contact.

AMORPHOUSNESS
The malleable body of a black pudding lets it squeeze through impossibly tiny gaps. Even an inch will do!

GELATINOUS CUBE

Gelatinous cubes travel through dungeon passages in silent, predictable patterns. They consume living flesh, but cannot dissolve bones or other materials. You can detect a well-fed cube by the bones and belongings of its recent victims, still suspended within the moving creature.

SPECIAL POWERS

ENGULFMENT
By moving into an individual's space, the gelatinous cube can engulf its target, completely surrounding it with ooze. Engulfed creatures are burned by the cube's acidic form and cannot breathe while inside.

TRANSPARENCY
A gelatinous cube is completely transparent, aside from any undigested remains from previous victims that it may contain. As a result, it is almost completely invisible when not moving.

GRAY OOZE

When still, gray ooze looks exactly like wet stone. This allows the ooze to blend perfectly with stone walls and floors, lying in wait for prey to pass. Only when it moves to attack does the gray ooze become visible, rising up like a liquid snake to strike at its intended victim. Like black pudding, gray ooze has corrosion and amorphousness powers.

OCHRE JELLY

These yellowish blobs slide under doors and through narrow cracks, and even crawl upside-down on the ceiling, in pursuit of food. They are just smart enough to avoid large groups, waiting for better odds before attacking. Like gelatinous cubes, ochre jelly can dissolve flesh but not bone, wood, metal, or other materials. They are immune to damage from lightning or sharp weapons.

ROPER

SPECIAL POWERS

GRAPPLING
Ropers can have up to six tendrils, which they use to grab their targets and pull them closer. Each tendril has hairlike protrusions that can penetrate a creature's skin and sap their strength, making escape even harder. If a tendril is cut off, the roper can regenerate a new one in its place.

SPIDER CLIMBING
Ropers can climb difficult surfaces with ease, including along walls and across ceilings. They move slowly but silently.

MULTI-ATTACK
A roper can make up to six attacks at once, including four tendril strikes, one bite, and one attempt to pull a target in close to them.

SIZE Ropers are typically between eight and sixteen feet long, about the size of a family car. They have up to six tendrils, a single eye, and dangerously sharp teeth.

Ropers are patient predators that mimic the rock protrusions of caves, pushing up from the ground or hanging down from above, waiting for prey to approach. Unlike real rocks, ropers can move (although slowly), sliding silently along until they are in the perfect position to attack. When still, ropers are indistinguishable from normal rocks.

When a roper attacks, its single eye opens and up to six tendrils lash out at the target. A wide mouth filled with jagged teeth snaps out to bite, while making terrible guttural sounds to intimidate prey. Ropers can digest almost anything, except platinum, gemstones, and magical items. Gruesome as it sounds, some adventurers have found great treasures by searching through a roper's stomach once it's dead!

LAIR Ropers are typically found in less-refined parts of a dungeon, such as natural caves or rough-hewn rooms. They can appear as either stalagmites, pushing up from the dungeon floor, or stalactites, hanging from above.

DO THIS

Attack with all you've got. Ropers may look like rock but they can be hurt by regular weapons. So stab, slash, and use magic to strike down these creatures as quick as you can.

Watch for moving rocks. Ropers will move into the best position before attacking; so when exploring caves, keep an eye out for rocks that change locations.

DON'T DO THIS

Don't relax (even after they're dead). Ropers make loud guttural noises while attacking, which can alert other creatures to investigate. Don't let your guard down too soon.

SEA ELF

1

SPECIAL POWERS

FRIEND OF THE SEA
Using gestures and sounds, sea elves can communicate simple ideas to ocean creatures, asking them to keep watch, retrieve small objects, or perform other simple tasks.

CHILD OF THE SEA
Sea elves can move quickly through water. They can breathe both air and water, moving at will between land and ocean environments.

SIZE Like their land-based cousins, sea elves are slightly slimmer and taller than humans. Their skin tone ranges from green to blue, and they have visible gills on their necks and chest.

Thousands of years ago, some members of the ancient race of elves turned their attention to the beauty of the sea and devoted their long lives to exploring its depths and understanding its varied mysteries. Through magical means, they developed the ability to live their entire lives underwater.

All elves share a love for nature, but sea elves have a special devotion to the sea. They make a point of befriending its many other inhabitants and exploring its murky shadows. Sea elves have learned secrets that no one on the shoreline may ever know!

Like all elves, sea elves can easily be friend or foe depending on the circumstances in which you encounter them. They tend to be reclusive, and the oceans are vast, so you may only ever meet a sea elf when some crisis forces them to the surface world.

LAIR As their name suggests, sea elves live beneath the ocean waves, usually in underwater caves or cities. They mainly reside in small hidden communities, which resonate with the beautifully eerie music unique to the sea elves.

DO THIS

Approach in peace. Sea elves specialize in ranged attacks. If they think you're approaching with bad intentions, you may end up on the wrong end of a trident!

Look out for sea creatures. Sea elves can communicate in very simple ways with aquatic animals, so sea creatures that are behaving strangely may be acting as spies for the sea elves.

DON'T DO THIS

Don't try to swim away. Sea elves are excellent and graceful swimmers and can breathe underwater. They'll catch up to you very quickly!

Don't pollute the sea. Sea elves care deeply about their home and do not take kindly to people who try to ruin it.

WATER ELEMENTAL MYRMIDON

3

SPECIAL POWERS

FREEZING STRIKE
This power adds a cold blast to normal trident attacks, doing extra damage and slowing down their target for a few seconds.

ELEMENTAL IMMUNITY
As elementals, myrmidons cannot be paralyzed, petrified, poisoned, or knocked over. They also take less damage from non-magical attacks, such as normal swords or arrows.

SIZE The size of a water elemental myrmidon is determined by the size of the magical plate mail into which it's bound. While giant-size myrmidons exist (and are terrifying), most are slightly larger than humans, although they can manipulate their watery form to appear taller.

Water elemental myrmidons are conjured by elemental power and shackled into specially created suits of plate mail armor by a complex magical ritual. They possess no memory of their former existence as free elementals bound to a specific water-filled location, such as a pool or a fountain, and must obey every command given by their creator.

Water elemental myrmidons carry magic three-pronged tridents that they can use to make melee attacks. They also have a freezing strike power that does additional cold damage when they land a hit with their trident.

LAIR As bound magical creatures, they live wherever their creator orders them to be, which is usually guarding an important location or valuable treasure. Most elementals must exist within or near to their element, but myrmidons are free from that restriction, since their plate mail armor serves as their personal lair.

DO THIS

Break out your magical attacks. Water elemental myrmidons are resistant to normal damage, so you'll need magical weapons and spells to win this fight.

Set them free. If you can break the spell that binds them to their armor, a free water elemental is likely to flee rather than keep fighting.

DON'T DO THIS

Don't try to poison them. Their watery bodies easily flush out any poisons, making them immune to such attacks.

Don't target their creator. The spell that binds a water elemental myrmidon to its armor won't break if you defeat the original spellcaster.

YIKARIA

1

SPECIAL POWERS

SKIN CRAWLING

Yikaria have the ability to take over someone else's body. Known as "skin crawling," this psychic attack allows them to control their victims' every action. Fortunately, the yikaria require at least an hour of constant physical contact to complete this process, so they can't take over one of your allies during a fight.

SIZE Yikarai resemble disgruntled yaks, if yaks stood on their two hind legs and wore primitive clothes. They're about as tall as an ostrich, but almost twice as heavy.

The yikaria, also known as yakfolk, are a race of hulking humanoids with faces, fur, and horns that resemble those of yaks. They live in remote hidden settlements that appear to visitors a lot like paradise due to the yikaria life of luxury and leisure.

In reality, yikaria culture is heartless and cruel, built on the backs of slaves. Any visitors who stumble into their enclaves are likely to find themselves in chains. By forcing others to do all their work, the yikaria are free to pursue their passion for dark magic and to dedicate themselves to the worship of a vile deity called the Forgotten God.

Among the dark powers the yikaria can tap into is an ability called "skin crawling," which allows them to take possession of the minds of other creatures by meditating for a short period while maintaining physical contact with their victim. Through this power, they can effectively turn an adventurer against their most trusted allies!

LAIR Yikaria prefer to live in somewhat remote areas, where there are few others to question the dark secret behind their seemingly idyllic communities. Their largest settlement is at Ironslag, where a yikaria village marks the main entrance to the mines, and a watermill powers the elevator that takes people into the forge below.

DO THIS

Keep out of sight. The safest way to deal with the yikaria is to never encounter them at all. When attacked, the yikaria often slaughter their slaves to prevent an uprising.

Stay awake. If you fall asleep in a yikaria enclave, you'll either end up a slave or be possessed by their skin-crawling powers.

DON'T DO THIS

Don't trust a yikari. Yikaria culture prizes deceit and betrayal. The kindest yikaria you meet will only be waiting for a chance to double-cross you.

Don't accept any food or drink. Anything they offer you is almost certainly poisoned.

BUILDING YOUR OWN DUNGEON

Traveling to remote dungeons and unlocking their secrets is rewarding, but even more exciting is the thrill of creating your own fiendish fortress or sunken stronghold. From initial idea to layout, treasure and traps, every part is yours to produce and populate.

When you close your eyes, what kind of dungeon do you see? Does it have ornate halls and spiral staircases, or are there twisting caverns made of rough-hewn rock? Is it a moss-covered ruin in a dense jungle, or a glittering ice-tower carved from a glacier?

In a world where magic and monsters are real, there are no limits, only new destinations to explore.

DUNGEON CONCEPT

When you set out to create your own dungeon, think about its function and the distinct features you can use to engage adventurers as they explore it. A goblin village isn't the same as a cloud giant's stronghold or a white dragon's lair. Each one would look different, feel different, and carry their own unique threats.

LOCATION

Figuring out where your dungeon is located will instantly start to narrow your focus and generate other ideas. Look to the following list of dungeon locales for inspiration, or come up with your own. The options are endless!

- Behind a waterfall
- Beneath a graveyard
- Floating in the sky
- In a cliff face
- In catacombs beneath a city
- In the desert
- Inside a volcano
- Underwater

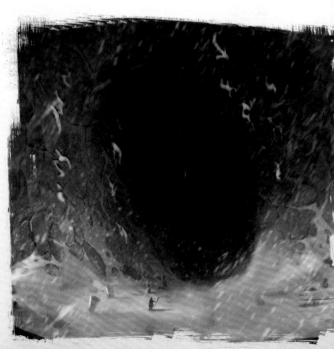

CREATOR

Knowing who built this dungeon will also help you understand the size and scope of the place you're creating. And remember, whomever constructed it doesn't still have to be dwelling there. Many dungeons are abandoned and reused over the centuries.

Use any of the following potential creator options, or come up with something of your own invention.

A forgotten civilization

A wizard

An evil cult

Dwarves

Elves

Goblins

Smugglers

No creator at all (natural formations)

PURPOSE

Dungeons are built to fulfill an objective. Knowing what that is will help you define important areas within. Also, keep in mind that dungeons can be repeatedly abandoned and then repurposed by different occupants. A shrine can fall into ruin and become a lair, or a castle may have been struck by a dark plague and become a tomb.

Death Trap: A way to guard treasure or a competition to test the skills of warriors and wizards alike, a death trap is built to destroy any who enter.

Lair: A monster's living quarters and also a place where it can hoard its valuables. Be careful, a creature confronted in its home tends to fight with even more intensity than usual.

Mine: An active mine where rare ore, gemstones, or metals are harvested, or an abandoned mine occupied by creatures who thrive in the dark.

Stronghold: A secure base of operations for villains or monsters. A fortress like this is built with defense in mind, so a successful delve may involve infiltration rather than charging at the front entrance.

Temple or Shrine: Whether still active or now abandoned, this place was intended for worship and ritual.

Tomb: A resting place for the departed, along with their secrets and treasures.

POPULATING YOUR DUNGEON

What's a dungeon without monsters to fight? Start by choosing a few of your favorite foes, then use the following guidelines to help decide on the rest.

ECOLOGY

Areas where people or creatures gather have their own ecosystems. Creatures who live there need to eat, drink, breathe, and sleep. A king needs a throne room, but also a bedroom. Worshippers need places to pray. Soldiers need barracks and storage areas for their equipment. Are there areas still under construction or that have been closed off due to collapse, mold, or other issues that have arisen? When you set out to design a dungeon, you should think about the internal logic of the spaces you're creating and what the occupants need in order to carry out their day-to-day tasks—food preparation will probably be close to food storage, a guardhouse should be near the prison cells it watches over, or a hatchery placed by the sleeping area of a protective mother.

INHABITANTS

A dungeon is sometimes dominated by a single monster or a large group of intelligent creatures, but they don't have to be the sole occupants. Fungi, vermin, scavengers, and various predators can all coexist in the same space with the main inhabitants.

- Do the creatures controlling this dungeon have pets? If so, where are those pets kept and how are they fed?

- Do the occupants of this place take prisoners? Are those captives potential allies to you if they're freed?

- If a dungeon is quite large, are there multiple factions within vying for control?

- The ways in which all the dungeon's inhabitants interact will give you any number of story ideas.

TRAPS

Intentional and dangerous, traps are created to fool the unwary and stop their progress through a dungeon. These devices may be built to hurt or to hold, but they're always constructed to cause trouble.

Like the dungeon itself, when creating traps you must first decide who built them and what purpose they serve. It's rare that a trap would be set up in a space where denizens need to travel often, so think carefully about why it's been placed there and what lies beyond that's worth protecting.

Second, decide if the trap will be mechanical or magical in nature. Mechanical traps include basic ambush material such as pits or falling blocks, but can ramp up in complexity to whirling blades, flying arrows, flooding rooms, or clockwork puzzles. Magical traps cast a spell when activated and the effects can be almost anything you imagine: A floor trap could teleport the person who sets it off to another part of the dungeon.

Third, determine how the trap is triggered, what the effect will be, and how a group of adventurers might detect it if they were careful enough: Opening a door improperly could prompt a blast of magical fire to erupt into the hallway. Intelligent creatures who place traps in their lairs need ways to get past them without harming themselves. A trap might have a secret switch that disables its effect or an alternate route that adventurers can take to bypass it entirely.

CATACOMBS

ONE SQUARE EQUALS 10 FEET

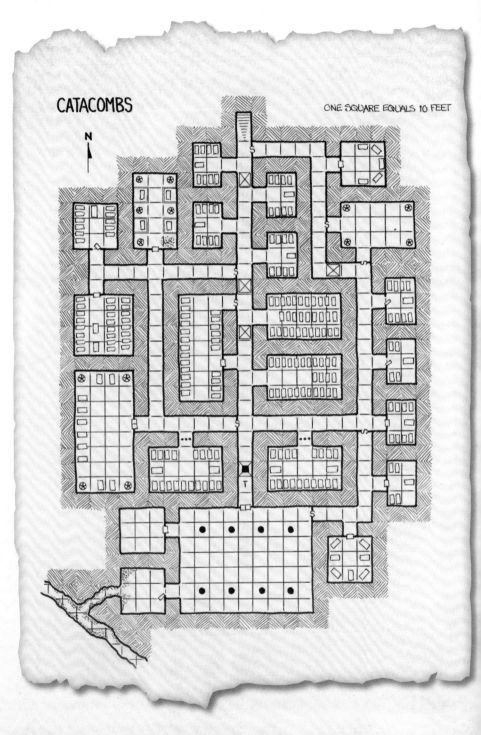

MAPMAKING

Having a concept, knowing the occupants, and creating a list of different areas are the perfect ingredients for building a dungeon. Now you need to start making a map!

A dungeon is most easily mapped on graph paper, with each square representing a standard measurement, such as five or ten feet per square. Use your key areas as starting points, then connect them with other features. As you plan, keep these points in mind.

- Symmetry is boring. If a group of adventurers explores one half of a dungeon, they'll rush through the second half if the layout is the same. Don't make your maps too predictable.

- Even if a dungeon is manually constructed, there are ways to incorporate indigenous features as well. Waterfalls, chasms, falling rocks, and other natural elements can provide interesting obstacles for your players.

- Using the grid is a nice way to get straight hallways and rectangular rooms, but don't be afraid to switch things up by varying the shape, size, and direction of your dungeon areas.

- Think about furniture and storage. How are the denizens using this space and what is needed to carry out daily tasks?

- Even though your map is two-dimensional, think in three dimensions. Use stairs, ramps, platforms, ledges, and balconies to add height or depth. It will make your dungeon more interesting than just having an endless series of level rooms.

- The ultimate goal within your dungeon will usually be as far from the entrance as possible, forcing adventurers deeper into danger and heightening the drama.

MAP SYMBOLS

Here are a series of standardized symbols you can use on your graph-paper maps to denote specific dungeon features. Mix and match them to bring to life the hidden places you've always imagined.

Symbol	Name	Symbol	Name
	DOOR		TRAPDOOR IN CEILING
	DOUBLE DOOR		TRAPDOOR IN FLOOR
	SECRET DOOR		SECRET TRAPDOOR
	ONE-WAY DOOR		OPEN PIT
	ONE-WAY SECRET DOOR		COVERED PIT
	FALSE DOOR		TRAP
	REVOLVING DOOR		STAIRS
	CONCEALED DOOR		STAIRS/SLIDE TRAP
	ARCHWAY		SPIRAL STAIRS
	OPEN DOORWAY		NATURAL STAIRS
	PORTCULLIS OR BARS		LADDER

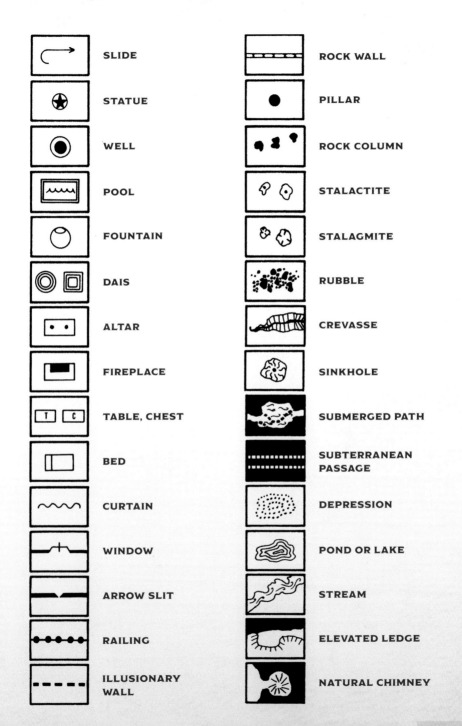

SLIDE	ROCK WALL
STATUE	PILLAR
WELL	ROCK COLUMN
POOL	STALACTITE
FOUNTAIN	STALAGMITE
DAIS	RUBBLE
ALTAR	CREVASSE
FIREPLACE	SINKHOLE
TABLE, CHEST	SUBMERGED PATH
BED	SUBTERRANEAN PASSAGE
CURTAIN	DEPRESSION
WINDOW	POND OR LAKE
ARROW SLIT	STREAM
RAILING	ELEVATED LEDGE
ILLUSIONARY WALL	NATURAL CHIMNEY

MAP EXAMPLES

The shrine of an evil cult where worshipers gather to make sacrifices, or a holy place of worship overrun by invading hordes that need to be cleared out by brave adventurers? You decide which one your adventuring party will face!

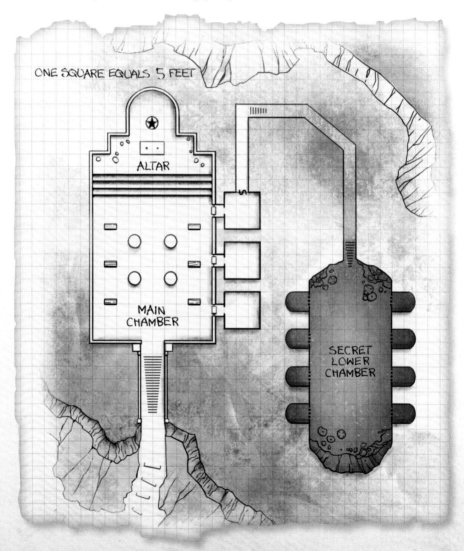

A haunted ship sailing through ghostly waters, or a pirate boat manned by cut-throat villains who have been terrorizing innocent farmers along the shoreline? Every map contains multiple possibilities, depending on how you decide to customize it!

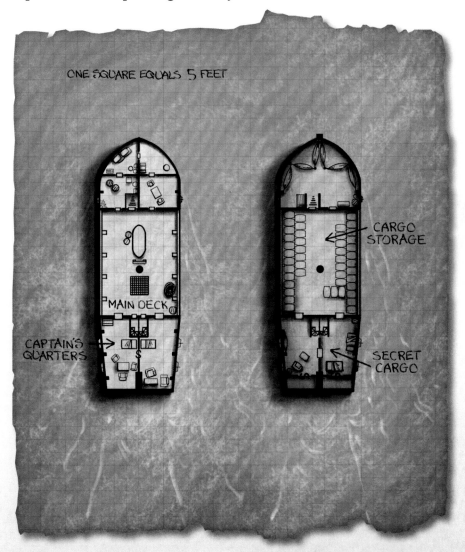

ONE SQUARE EQUALS 5 FEET

MAIN DECK

CAPTAIN'S QUARTERS

CARGO STORAGE

SECRET CARGO

EXPLORATION & QUESTS

How a dungeon experience begins and how it ends can contribute a great deal to making the journey through the space a memorable one. Epic fantasy stories don't start with someone merely opening a door and walking down a hallway. Use the entrance of your dungeon as a way to set expectations and to build excitement about the dangers and delights that lay ahead.

- What kind of journey is required to get to the dungeon? Is it close by or in a remote and inhospitable location?

- Is the entrance hidden? If so, what clues or methods must the adventurers use to find it?

- Is the entrance guarded? Who watches over this space and what will it take to get past them?

- Is the entrance locked? Is there a key, a magical phrase, or a trick used to gain access?

- Is the entrance magical? A teleportation circle may transport adventurers directly into the heart of a dungeon, or a permanent illusion may hide the safest entrance to a creature's lair.

- Is there more than one entrance? A fortress has a main gate, but there may be other smaller entry points for servants, shipping, or garbage disposal that adventurers can use to make their way inside. A cave may have a large opening at the base of a mountain, but there may be smaller tunnels at higher points as well.

Once a group has plumbed the depths of your dungeon, you'll want to make sure the final encounter is worthy of their time and effort. What kind of big set piece can you use and what foes can they face that will engage and excite them? What final obstacle must they overcome for their quest to be declared a success?

Are there any other tasks you can add to the final encounter beyond merely fighting a villain? Freeing prisoners, stopping a ritual, activating an ancient artifact, or undoing a curse can split the adventuring party's attention in a way that feels frantic and exciting. Maybe the final battle ends with the entire room crumbling as the floor gives way, sending the heroes plummeting toward an underground river that threatens to wash them away. Whatever you decide, make it exciting; because if you do, you and your friends can build stories together that you'll always remember.

TREASURE

At the end of every quest there must be a reward, a reason for adventurers to go through trials and tribulations while risking their health and happiness. For a cleric, that reward may be a renewal of faith after serving the needs of their deity. For a paladin, it may come in the form of pride from vanquishing evil. Along with satisfaction, conviction, and an overall sense of a job well done, the most common and appreciated form of compensation in a world of sword and sorcery is treasure. When you build your dungeon and populate it with dangers aplenty, you'll also want to decide what kind of wealth is available for plundering. Here are some ideas to get you started.

Art Objects: Idols or other sculptures, paintings, rare musical instruments, and even finely crafted dinnerware may be found and have value.

Coins: Simple and to the point. Gold, silver, and copper coins are the most common, but there are also rarer electrum and platinum ones to be considered as well.

Gemstones: Diamonds, rubies, sapphires, emeralds, amethysts, and dozens of other gems, plus brand-new crystal fascinations you come up with from your own imagination.

Jewelry: Necklaces, earrings, rings, bracelets, and other trinkets. Some may be kept and worn by adventurers while others can be traded or sold.

Knowledge: Rare books or scrolls, spell books, or alchemic recipes. For researchers and spellcasters, there may be information worth more than mere gold can purchase.

Magic Items: Wondrous items and enchanted objects are the kind of treasure many adventurers crave. Create your own or look to the *Wizards & Spells* guide for specific items to use.

New Adventure: A map to another destination, a mysterious code to be solved, or a journal detailing a villainous plot—sometimes the most valuable thing an explorer can find is a reason to keep exploring.

HOW MUCH IS TOO MUCH?

Receiving riches is a thrill, but be careful not to overload your dungeon with too much treasure. Magical items are less enchanting if a hero has a backpack full of them, and the desire to take on new expeditions can fade quickly if characters have more money than they know what to do with.

Keep in mind that the life of an adventurer does come with financial obligations. Armor needs to be repaired, clothes replaced, and weapons sharpened, and there are always local peasants in need who could use some of that newly unearthed gold to better their own lots in life. As a hero's legend begins to grow, their needs and expenses will rise to match their reputation.

USING DUNGEONS
TO TELL YOUR OWN STORIES

"The door is made of thick oak and reinforced with bands of metal."

"Is there a keyhole?"

"There is."

"Okay, Khylie will pull out her thieves' tools and spring that lock."

"Hold on a sec. I'm gonna shoulder-check the door and bust it open. We don't have time to sit around while she messes with finicky locks."

"Are you sure?"

"Yeah, absolutely. Dorbo tucks his head down, gets a running start, and charges at the door."

"I never actually said the door was locked . . . so you smash into the door and it instantly flies open. You're running full speed and weren't expecting it to give way so easily, so now you can't stop."

"Uh oh."

"You stumble a few feet, trip, and fall to the floor right in the middle of nine skeletons armed with rusty swords who were waiting for you on the other side. Their bones click and grind as they move in to attack."

Now that you've put together your own dungeon concept and sketched out a map, you're well on your way to becoming a Dungeon Master! What matters most is using your imagination and collaborating with your friends to create something new that you wouldn't have been able to come up with on your own.

Your idea might start with a one dungeon, but it can go *anywhere*: a creature's lair, the village nearby, cities and castles, caverns or skyscapes. You get to choose all the ingredients and stir them together. To help you as you develop your story, here are some questions to keep in mind:

WHO ARE YOUR CHARACTERS?

- Are your heroes like you or different? Young or old, human or something else? Think about the foes you must face. Great heroes require great challenges. What makes your villains memorable and powerful, and what brings them into conflict with your adventurers?

WHERE DOES YOUR STORY TAKE PLACE?

- At the top of a mountain, in a serene forest, deep underwater, or in a creepy boneyard?

WHEN DOES THE STORY HAPPEN?

- At night or during the day, in the middle of a thunderstorm or right before the bells toll to ring in the new year? Think about time passing as your story unfolds.

HOW DO THINGS CHANGE AS THE STORY PROCEEDS?

- Do your heroes succeed or fail? Do they find somewhere new or explore someplace old?

WHAT SHOULD SOMEONE FEEL AS THEY EXPERIENCE YOUR STORY?

- Do you want them to laugh or get scared? Cheer or be grossed out?

WHY ARE YOUR HEROES GOING ON THIS ADVENTURE?

- Knowing what their goals are will help you create a compelling tale of heroism and exploration.

Remember, you don't have to answer all these questions by yourself! DUNGEONS & DRAGONS is a collaborative game where you work with your friends to create your own stories. One person acts as a narrator, called a Dungeon Master, and the other players each take on the role of a hero, called a Player Character, in the adventuring party in a story. The Dungeon Master sets up a scene by describing a place and any threats that may exist, and then each player contributes ideas by explaining their own character's actions. With each scene created by the group, the story moves forward in unexpected and entertaining ways.

If you don't feel confident starting from scratch, you can go to your local gaming store and play a DUNGEONS & DRAGONS demonstration session. Demos can be a quick way to learn how the game is played and an opportunity to possibly make some brand-new friends at the same time.

After you've read through all the environs in this little dungeon document, there's even more DUNGEONS & DRAGONS material to ignite your imagination. The *Monsters & Creatures* guide is bursting at the seams with beasts aplenty for you and your friends to defeat. *Warriors & Weapons* goes into more detail about the different adventuring races and the martial classes who can join you on your quest. And the *Wizards & Spells* guide is filled with mystical magic to aid in your exploits. You know what dangerous places are to be found out there in the darkness, now figure out who your hero will be and *go forth on an adventure!*

Published in the United States by Ten Speed Press, an imprint of Random House, a division of Penguin Random House LLC, New York.
www.crownpublishing.com
www.tenspeed.com

Ten Speed Press and the Ten Speed Press colophon are registered trademarks of Penguin Random House LLC.

Originally published in the United States in hardcover by Ten Speed Press, an imprint of Random House, a division of Penguin Random House LLC, New York, in 2019.

Publisher: Aaron Wehner
Art Director and Designer: Betsy Stromberg
Editors: Patrick Barb and Julie Bennett
Managing Editor: Doug Ogan
Production Designer: Lisa Bieser
Wizards of the Coast Team: David Gershman, Kate Irwin, Adam Lee, Hilary Ross, Liz Schuh
Illustrations: Conceptopolis, LLC

10 9 8 7

2020 Trade Paperback Boxed Set Edition

MONSTERS & CREATURES

DUNGEONS & DRAGONS®

MONSTERS & CREATURES

A Young Adventurer's Guide

WRITTEN BY JIM ZUB

WITH STACY KING AND ANDREW WHEELER

TEN SPEED PRESS
California | New York

CONTENTS

INTRODUCTION

Monsters are freaky. Creatures can be fun. Both make our stories exciting and dangerous.

This book is a tour through some of the most famous and frightening beasts from the world of DUNGEONS & DRAGONS. It's a guide to their traits, lairs, and powers. It will tell you how to fight these weird creatures or advise you when to flee if you're in over your head.

Read this book from start to finish, or open it to any spot, get entranced by the cool artwork, and start your journey there. The more you read, the more you'll discover. The more you discover, the easier it will be to imagine your own heroic tales as you explore strange caves, trek across craggy mountains, or soar through the skies.

Will your battles against these monsters lead to fame and fortune or will your skeleton lie as an omen for future heroes to discover? In the end, that's up to you. DUNGEONS & DRAGONS is all about unique adventures, and yours is about to begin.

Enjoy!

DANGER LEVELS

Each monster profile includes a number indicating the danger level of that creature, with a **0** being harmless, a **1** as a reasonable threat for a beginning adventurer, and building up from there. A **5** is incredibly dangerous and requires an experienced group of adventurers to possibly defeat it. There are some **epic** creatures more powerful than a mere number can define. Such terrors can only be fought by legendary heroes armed with the most powerful magic weapons and spells imaginable.

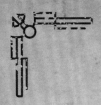

CAVERNS & DARK PLACES

In the earth beneath your feet, things are *moving*.

Creatures of all shapes and sizes burrow through dirt and stone, muck and clay. Vast tunnels connect to winding caves, and inside those flow rivers that have never seen the sun. In places such as the Underdark, entire kingdoms of intelligent creatures can be found.

Some of these subterranean spaces are cool and wet, with condensation dripping from above. Others are hot and steamy, with a thin wall of rock serving as your only protection from streams of burning magma that bubble up from a molten core.

The underground is a place of darkness and danger, where hidden treasures can be found in a hole and a sputtering torch is your only source of light. Are you ready to go exploring?

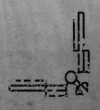

BEHOLDER

4

SPECIAL POWERS Beholders have one big eyeball in the center of their round bodies and ten weird eyestalks. Each eyestalk has a magic beam that shoots at adventurers when angry.

TELEKINESIS
This eye's beam can hold you in place or move you around.

DISINTEGRATION
This eye's beam turns whatever it hits to dust.

PETRIFICATION
One hit from this eye's beam will turn a living creature into stone.

SLEEP
This eye's beam can make you so tired that you fall asleep on the spot. No pillow. No blanket. Just naptime.

ENERVATION
This eye's spell hurts like a bad burn.

DEATH
Yikes!

SLOWNESS
If this eye's beam hits you, then you'll move really slowly, like you're trying to run underwater.

FEAR
If this eye's spell works its magic, you'll find yourself running away because of uncontrollable fear.

PARALYZATION
If you get hit with this one, you won't be able to move at all for a full minute. Count to sixty and hope you still have time to run afterward.

CHARM
If you fall under this eye's spell, you'll think the beholder is your friend and do what it says.

ANTIMAGIC CONE
Wherever this eye looks, magic won't work. Clerics, wizards, and warlocks, try to stay out of its sight.

Beholders are freaky floating creatures with shimmering eyes that cast evil spells. Is that big blob the beholder's head or its body? Are those eyestalks coming out of the top its hair or its limbs? There are no easy answers. All you need to know is that a beholder is a scary floating eyeball monster. And if any of those eyes set their gaze on you, you're in big trouble.

Beholders are jealous, angry creatures. They have such a bad attitude that they don't even get along with each other (which is actually a good thing because if you found more than one at the same time you'd probably be a goner).

LAIR Most beholders live in remote places such as caves or abandoned ruins. Some of them even build their own lairs by disintegrating rock with their eye blasts in order to create tall tunnels where they can float above their prey and cause trouble. The floor of a beholder's cave is usually covered with treasure and equipment from unfortunate adventurers who didn't think to look up when they walked in the entrance.

SIZE Some beholders are small like a basketball, but older ones can be massive, more than ten feet in diameter, like a humongous beachball.

DO THIS	DON'T DO THIS
Fight magic with magic. If your party includes spellcasters, get them to put up magical shields to protect your fighters from the beholder's eye beams.	**Don't ignore the feeling that you're being watched.** Even when you're alone, feeling someone's eyes on you is a sign that a beholder may be close by.
Distract the beholder as much as you can. Give it a lot of different things to look at so that it won't see you.	**Don't stay put for too long!** Holding your ground may be a great fighting tactic against some monsters, but not against beholders. If those eyes focus on you, it's bad news.
Get in close! Beholders are most dangerous when they're far away because they can shoot their eye beams at you and your party.	

BUGBEAR

1

SPECIAL POWERS

BRUTE STRENGTH
Close combat weapons do extra damage when wielded by these ferocious fighters.

HEART OF HRUGGEK
Named after a bugbear god, bugbear chiefs can call upon this formidable power to shrug off attacks intended to charm, frighten, paralyze, poison, or stun them.

SURPRISE ATTACK
An explosive burst of power allows a bugbear to inflict even more damage during its first strike, raising its danger level, if it manages to catch you off guard.

SIZE Bugbears are a little taller than a normal doorway, with broad shoulders and thick, muscular limbs. Their abnormally long arms give them extra reach for melee attacks.

Bugbears are fierce warriors born for battle and mayhem! Much larger than their goblin cousins (see page 12), bugbears like to bully and boss other creatures around. They will fight for others if their employer promises enough gold and carnage to satisfy their barbaric tastes. However, even a well-paid bugbear is an unreliable ally. Covered in thick fur that they enhance with hide armor, they favor brutal weapons such as the morning star, a spiked mace.

Bugbears are fond of ambushes and are surprisingly stealthy for their size. They are often found in the company of goblins whom they have enslaved or rule over with brutal force (though they do sometimes unite to form war bands led by a particularly strong warrior). Beneath their fierce exteriors, bugbears are cowards who will abandon wounded members of their parties and flee when the fight turns against them. A wounded bugbear has no qualms about betraying his former allies if it will help save his own hide!

LAIR Like goblins, bugbears favor dismal settings such as caves, abandoned mines, and rotting dungeons. Some simply move into goblin lairs and take over! You may sometimes find war bands rampaging through rocky terrain or anywhere that treasure and conquests can be found.

DO THIS

Stay out of reach. Bugbears' long arms give them an advantage in close combat, so use ranged attacks when possible.

Take captives. Bugbears will sell out their tribe and allies for a chance at survival.

DON'T DO THIS

Don't ignore their goblin companions. The smaller creatures may be less dangerous one-on-one, but a goblin horde presents a risk for even the most accomplished adventurer.

Don't let down your guard. Known for their stealth, bugbears love to attack when they're least expected. Stay alert!

CARRION CRAWLER

SPECIAL POWERS

SENSE OF SMELL
Carrion crawlers have an amazing sense of smell that lets them sniff out prey from far away. That also makes it tough to sneak up on them.

CLIMBING
Their many legs allow them to climb like a spider, skittering over difficult surfaces and even moving while upside down.

POISON
Their tentacles carry a poison that can paralyze you. Once you can't move, the carrion crawler will tuck you away to let you die and rot until you're gooey enough to be its next meal.

Carrion crawlers are huge caterpillar-like creatures, each with dozens of tentacles and a gnashing mouth full of razor-sharp teeth. These disgusting monsters live on rotting flesh and slimy bones, and they're always on the hunt for their next meal.

Carrion crawlers are drawn to dead things. They follow the stench of death and decay like relentless bloodhounds. These patient predators rely on trickery to fill their ever-hungry bellies. Unwary adventurers face the risk of being grabbed and poisoned by one of their many tentacles or bitten by their snapping teeth.

LAIR Carrion crawlers are found in caves, sewers, dungeons, and marshlands—anywhere that's dark and moldy. Their keen sense of smell can sometimes lead them to cemeteries or battlefields. The dark corners of their lairs may contain the paralyzed or rotting corpses of their victims, stashed away for a late-night snack.

SIZE A fully grown carrion crawler is three times as long as a human is tall and almost six feet high when they crawl around. However, they can rear up on their hind-tentacles in combat to make themselves even taller, so watch out!

DO THIS	DON'T DO THIS
Be ready to cure poisonous wounds. Party members with healing powers, like clerics and druids, should be ready to help if anyone is struck by a poisonous tentacle.	**Don't make lots of noise while you move through the underground.** These relentless hunters will stalk you for hours in hopes of a meal.
Clean your weapons after a fight. Carrion crawlers can smell even a tiny hint of blood from miles away.	**Don't ignore what's above.** Carrion crawlers can move across ceilings just as easily as they can the ground, and they love to surprise their victims from above.

FLUMPH

SPECIAL POWERS

ADVANCED TELEPATHY
These powerful psychics can overhear the content of any telepathic communication within sixty feet.

TELEPATHIC SHROUD
Flumphs are immune to all attempts to read their thoughts or emotions against their will.

STENCH SPRAY
Flumphs can shoot a fifteen-foot-long cone of foul-smelling liquid that sticks to targets, leaving them stinking for hours.

ACID BURN
Flumphs can attack with their tendrils, which give off an acid that can burn skin.

Not everything that lurks in the dark is dangerous! Flumphs are one of the great oddities of the underground, peaceful little creatures who float through the darkness on puffs of air. They communicate telepathically and express their moods through the soft, glowing colors of their tentacles: soft pink for amusement, deep blue for sadness, green for curiosity, and red for anger.

Flumphs feed off the psychic energy of others. They are passive parasites who take only as much as needed for survival. Their telepathy exposes them to the evil thoughts and emotions of other underground dwellers, sickening their pure nature. When good-hearted adventurers approach, flumphs are eager to soak up the positive energy and share any dark secrets they have learned. A steadfast rule of underground exploration is to always trust a flumph!

LAIR Flumphs live in the Underdark and can typically be found near the lairs of mind flayers and other psionic creatures. Their own communities, called cloisters, are peaceful places where their telepathy allows them to live in perfect harmony.

SIZE An adult flumph has a circumference wider than a person, but is only about as thick as your arm, giving it an odd and flat saucer-shaped appearance.

DO THIS

Let them into your head. Flumphs can't speak, but they can share secrets and warnings via telepathy.

Keep an eye on their colors. Flumphs are angered by the presence of evil, so when they start to glow red, something bad is nearby.

DON'T DO THIS

Don't frighten them. Dungeons are stinky enough without being coated with a flumph's stench spray.

GOBLIN

1/3

GOBLIN POLITICS

Lairs are ruled by the strongest or smartest goblin, who must constantly fight to hold their position. Turnover among goblin bosses is high, since all goblins want to seize power for themselves! Many goblin tribes are ruled by bugbears (see page 6), who use their superior strength and size to bully their smaller cousins into submission.

SIZE Goblins are about the height of a kitchen table. They are short but stocky, which gives them better balance when moving across rocky or uneven terrain.

Goblins are small, black-hearted, and selfish creatures with an individually low danger rating—which is why they're almost always found in packs, often in numbers so great that they can simply overwhelm their enemies! These malicious creatures long for power and cannot help but celebrate whenever they have the upper hand. Lazy and undisciplined, they make poor servants and rely on alarms rather than guards to protect their lairs.

Goblins have an affinity for rats, which serve as pets, and wolves, whom they train as mounts. They prefer ambushes and hit-and-run attacks over straightforward battle. When alone, they are more likely to run away than challenge a stronger foe—but they can be dangerous when they band together! Goblins fight with scimitars and shortbows, and wear leather armor stolen from fallen enemies. Even with a leader, their infighting never stops. Goblins live to abuse, and they will turn on one another if no external target is available (a trait that adventurers can use to their advantage).

LAIR You'll find goblins in old caves, abandoned mines, derelict dungeons, and other forsaken places. They take advantage of their small size by riddling their lairs with tunnels and bolt-holes that block the passage of larger enemies. Goblins also set many traps and alarms to ensure they aren't caught unaware.

DO THIS

Target the leader. Goblins are cowardly and often run away once their strongest fighter is defeated.

Stay alert! Goblins favor ambushes and sneak attacks from behind, so beware when traveling through their territories.

Put on a fearsome show. Sometimes all it takes is a magic illusion or a powerful battle cry to send them scurrying.

DON'T DO THIS

Don't rush into battle. Goblin lairs are riddled with traps and alarms. Be careful to avoid setting them off.

Don't trust them! Goblins are habitual liars and cannot be trusted to keep their promises (unless their lives are on the line).

MIND FLAYER

SPECIAL POWERS

DOMINATE MONSTER
Overpowers the mind of any living creature, turning them into a psychic slave willing to give their own life for their master.

MIND BLAST
A psychic attack that batters heroes with powerful mental energy, leaving them stunned.

PSYCHIC STRIKE
Their tentacles can deliver damaging blows using psychic power and snare you in a tight grasp.

BRAIN EXTRACTION
A mighty attack, which works against already-stunned foes, allows the mind flayer to crack open enemy skulls and devour their brains.

SIZE Adult mind flayers are only slightly larger than normal humans. (It's their psychic powers, not their size, that make them deadly!) Elder brains are around ten feet in diameter.

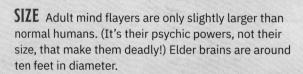

Wherever they appear, mind flayers are the scourge of sentient creatures. Psychic overlords and slavers, they are sinister masterminds that will not hesitate to wipe out entire races to achieve their own evil ends. Once, their empires oppressed many worlds; even today, their mental powers allow them to enact far-reaching schemes of intense cruelty.

The four tentacles on the squidlike head of a mind flayer are channels for their psychic powers. Mind flayers communicate telepathically, both among themselves and with the creatures they have psychically enslaved. Solitary mind flayers are rare, as most belong to colonies, each of which serves an elder brain. When a loyal mind flayer dies, its brain is harvested and deposited in the briny pool where the elder brain resides, so their gray matter and knowledge can be absorbed by their leader. A mind flayer's mental control is so absolute that their slaves will battle to the death to protect their master!

LAIR Mind flayers reside within the Underdark, a vast network of subterranean tunnels and caves that lies below the earth. They live in colonies of five or more adults who are all related to the elder brain that lives in a briny pool near the middle of their den. Mind flayers acting alone are outcasts, and often gather mind-controlled slaves around themselves for added security.

DO THIS

Aim for the brain. Despite its impressive mental attacks, the elder brain is relatively defenseless compared to an adult mind flayer.

Watch out for others. Mind flayers rarely live alone, so look out for siblings or enslaved creatures.

Starve them out. Mind flayers eat humanoid brains to survive. Cut off their food supply to weaken them before your final attack.

DON'T DO THIS

Don't focus on their slaves. If you can kill the mind flayer, you'll break its control—and freed slaves are more likely to run than continue attacking.

Don't let down your guard. It will take all of your focus not to fall prey to the mind flayer's psychic powers.

MYCONID

SPECIAL POWERS

DISTRESS SPORES

When hurt, a myconid releases special spores that alert other myconids within two hundred forty feet of its pain.

PACIFYING SPORES

These spores can stun a single target near the myconid, allowing the pacifist creature to avoid combat.

RAPPORT SPORES

All creatures within a thirty-foot radius are bound together in a telepathic link that allows them to communicate silently for one hour.

ANIMATING SPORES

Produced by myconid sovereigns, these spores reanimate the corpses of living creatures, transforming them into loyal servants.

SIZE

SPROUT

All myconids begin life as sprouts, two to three feet tall, which gradually grow to adult size. They are relatively defenseless, but capable of wielding small melee weapons.

ADULT

Adults are six- to seven-foot-tall plant creatures capable of defending themselves with pacifying spores that stun opponents.

SOVEREIGN

At more than ten feet tall, these are the largest of all myconids. Sovereigns can reanimate dead creatures to do their bidding!

Myconids are intelligent, mobile fungi who resemble mushrooms, if mushrooms were shaped sort of like humans. These strange, intelligent creatures live in a sprawling subterranean kingdom called the Underdark, seeking enlightenment through communal mind-melds they create using their specialized spores.

If approached peacefully, myconids will allow adventurers safe passage through their colonies. They dislike violence, but are more than capable of defending themselves if attacked. Their spores can create psychic connections with other creatures and signal distress, induce calm, and even—in the case of their mighty sovereigns— reanimate the bodies of small- to large-size creatures. These loyal spore servants will not hesitate to defend their myconid masters from intruding adventurers, so be careful!

LAIR Myconids live in the Underdark and have darkvision, which allows them to move freely through the inky blackness of their homes. Each colony is made up of twenty or so myconid adults and a handful of their child sprouts, overseen by a powerful sovereign who is the largest in the colony.

DO THIS

Ask for help! These peaceful, intelligent creatures can be useful allies, sharing valuable knowledge of the area around their colony and the dangers that lie ahead.

Let the sunshine in! As dwellers of the Underdark, myconids can be weakened and even killed by exposure to sunlight. Maybe your party's magic-users have a spell that could help light up the darkness!

DON'T DO THIS

Don't think that a scarf over your nose will save you! Spores can be absorbed through the smallest patch of bare skin.

Don't brag about your conquests. Myconids despise violence!

MYCONID COLONY

Tulra shivered as the strange spores settled into her skin. Everything about the Underdark was unsettling, but the myconid colonies, with their eerie silence and musty, alien smells, were her least favorite. Still, the myconids had insight into the mind flayer known as Deenarh—knowledge she needed if she was to have any hope of breaking its dark hold over her village.

A shudder ran along Tulra's spine as the spores did their work, opening her up to the thoughts of the creatures around her. A dozen minds sparkled along the telepathic link, one brighter than the rest.

"We know you, barbarian," said the sovereign, its voice nothing but a psychic rattle in Tulra's head. "You smell like the half-orc who burnt down our colonies at Shilmista three summers past."

Tulra froze. The power of the myconid mind-meld was legendary, but she hadn't expected to be identified hundreds of miles from Shilmista. The revelation left her with a difficult choice. She could explain the terrible situation that led to the colony's demise and hope for forgiveness or lie and say it wasn't her—a difficult task given the psychic bond that linked their minds together.

Should Tulra tell a dangerous truth or a dangerous lie? If she chooses the truth, would the myconid colony offer her forgiveness or use their dangerous spores to seek revenge? If she lies, will the myconids detect her deception—and how would they react to discovering her untruth? It's up to you!

LEGENDARY MONSTER

DEMOGORGON

EPIC

SPECIAL POWERS Demogorgon can use his huge tentacles or tail to grab heroes and smash them. He can also cast powerful magic spells, but his most potent abilities come from the glowing eyes of his twin ape heads. With just a glance, Demogorgon can cause heroes to stop in their tracks or go crazy.

BEGUILING GAZE
Stuns you so you can't move or think as long as you're staring at him.

HYPNOTIC GAZE
Lets Demogorgon take control, making you do whatever he chooses if your mind isn't strong enough to resist.

INSANITY GAZE
Unravels your mind so your thoughts don't make any sense. Confused and dizzy, you won't be able to attack or communicate with anyone else.

Demogorgon is a horrific demon prince who epitomizes the forces of chaos. His massive body is a warped mixture of different creatures all jammed together: the legs, feet, and tail of a dinosaur; the tentacles of a giant octopus; and the upper body of an ape, with a pair of disturbing-looking apelike heads mounted on top, hungry and roaring. Demogorgon is one of the most dangerous creatures anywhere. A battle with him is either the well-planned culmination of a massive quest, or a suicidal fool's run that ends in annihilation.

Demogorgon embodies madness and destruction, and he constantly works to destroy order and goodness in the universe. The turmoil around Demogorgon helps empower him, but it's also a source of weakness. His two heads (named Aameul and Hathradiah) constantly argue about how best to destroy his foes, as his evil plans shift and change. It's hard to raise an army and plunge the world into chaos when your own two heads can rarely agree on how best to do it.

LAIR Demogorgon lives in a strange other dimension called the Abyss. The Abyss is a shifting and turbulent place of war and insanity, where only the most powerful adventurers could even have a chance to survive, let alone triumph. The Abyss is broken up into more than six hundred layers of dangerous lands, some of them without any ground to walk on, others without any air to breathe. On the Abyssal layer called the Gaping Maw, Demogorgon's fortress is partially submerged in dark and deadly water.

Traveling to the Abyss and confronting Demogorgon directly is almost impossible for anyone less than the most epic of heroes. Most battles with Demogorgon take place elsewhere, when the Prince of Demons chooses to travel to other worlds.

SIZE Demogorgon is eighteen feet tall, which means he could look into the second-story window of a multistory house. Each of his tentacles is wider than your whole body, and his ape mouths are large enough to bite you in half without even chewing.

FORESTS, MOUNTAINS & OTHER TERRAIN

Open fields. Gentle hills. Quiet forests. These are the lands where many people make their homes, living peaceful lives of farming and trade, communities large and small connected by interweaving roads.

But people are not the only ones who flock to such terrain. Rocky hills and shallow caves provide promising lairs for brutal beasts. Roadside obstructions allow ambushers to set upon unwary travelers. Even open plains may make a suitable home for the clever and the quick.

Though open sky may feel less oppressive than the claustrophobic dark of an underground lair, the creatures who prowl beneath the sun and stars are no less dangerous than the subterranean variety. Are you prepared to take on monsters who threaten the safety of peaceful communities across the land?

CENTAUR

THE WISDOM OF CENTAURS You might never encounter centaurs out in the wild, as they prefer to travel through remote lands. However, if they are too old or weak to travel, a lone centaur may end up living in a humanoid settlement. These noble individuals are often revered in the community for their knowledge of the world and ability to read natural omens.

SIZE The horse part of a centaur is about the same size and height of a large and powerful horse, but the human half of a centaur adds to its overall height, making these very imposing creatures to face in battle.

The proud nomadic race of creatures known as centaurs combine the speed and strength of horses with the determination and intelligence of humans. Their upper bodies allow them to wield weapons for hunting or warfare, while their lower bodies allow them to traverse great distances at tremendous speed or to trample an enemy underfoot.

Centaurs are tribal creatures who move along the same ancient trading routes used for generations, through lush forests, snow-capped mountains, and dry deserts, capturing or trading whatever supplies they need as they go. As they have no territory to defend, they are not naturally inclined toward war, but they still train for it, and are powerful and ferocious warriors when crossed.

Yet centaurs prefer a peaceful life, living in harmony with nature. They have tremendous respect for the cycles of the natural world, taking only what they need and giving back what they can.

LAIR Centaurs do not have lairs. They only settle in one place when forced to do so by injury or age. If you encounter a group of centaurs by an oasis or a lake one day, they will be gone the next, leaving little behind except hoofprints in the mud.

DO THIS

Keep your distance. Centaurs do not enjoy company, and they can strike fast if you venture too close.

Offer knowledge and seek their advice. Centaurs are well-traveled and value the knowledge gained from exploration; scholarly party members, like wizards and monks, may make an ally by offering a trade of information.

DON'T DO THIS

Don't mistake them for horses. Centaurs are not steeds for you to ride and will resent any remarks that insult their intelligence.

Don't pick a fight. Centaurs don't like to start fights, but they know how to finish them.

DISPLACER BEAST

SPECIAL POWERS

VERSATILE ASSAULTS
Their spiked tentacles hit like melee weapons and move independently, giving the displacer beast multiple options for attack.

DISPLACEMENT
Via magical illusion, the displacer beast appears to stand several feet away from its real location, making it difficult to both hit and avoid. If you do land a blow, this power is temporarily knocked out, giving you a better chance to win.

DARKVISION
Wicked, glowing eyes can pierce up to sixty feet (even through total darkness).

SIZE
Displacer beasts are one-and-a-half times the size of a panther, the great cat they most resemble. With six legs, their bodies are long and lean.

Displacer beasts are vicious magical monsters that possess the otherworldly ability to displace light so that they appear to be several feet away from their actual location. This power makes them dangerous opponents, since it's hard to fight enemies who are never quite where they seem to be. They resemble sleek predatory cats covered in blue-black fur, with six legs and two spiked tentacles sprouting from their shoulders. Their eyes glow with a deep malice, a fire that cannot be dimmed even in death.

Originally bred by the Unseelie Fae (dark faeries) to hunt unicorns, pegasi, and other marvelous creatures, displacer beasts soon escaped and spread across the lands. They retain a love for the hunt, killing for sport as well as for food, and may toy with weaker prey before making a final strike. They hunt alone or in small packs, using their wicked intelligence to set up ambushes for unwary travelers. Don't let these dangerous creatures catch you by surprise!

LAIR Whether solo or in packs, displacer beasts favor densely wooded areas near roadways, where they can easily ambush prey. They can sometimes be found alongside intelligent evil creatures, such as vampire lords or mind flayers, serving as guards within their lairs.

DO THIS

Aim wide. Their displacement ability means these wicked beasts are never where they seem to be.

Be alert for tricks. Displacer beasts are cunning creatures, favoring strategy over straightforward assault.

DON'T DO THIS

Don't chase after a retreating displacer beast. It may be trying to lure you toward the rest of its pack!

Don't stick to a schedule. Displacer beasts are clever enough to remember the schedules of travelers passing by on a regular basis, so avoid an ambush by changing up when and how you travel.

OWLBEAR

2

SPECIAL POWERS

KEEN SIGHT AND SMELL
Owlbears have exceptionally good vision, even in the dark, and are skilled at sniffing out prey. You'll need to be extra-stealthy to avoid detection.

DEADLY FEROCITY
Stubborn and ferocious, nothing frightens away an owlbear. They will keep fighting long after a more sensible creature would have run away.

MULTIATTACK
These dangerous creatures can attack twice in the time it takes most monsters to strike once, biting with their sharp beaks and slashing with their deadly claws all at the same time.

SIZE Owlbears are slightly larger than a grizzly bear, weighing more than 500 pounds, and standing about three and a half feet tall when on all fours. They are almost seven feet long and tower over humans and even elves when standing on their hind legs.

Part giant owl, part enormous bear, these vicious creatures are densely muscled and covered in thick feathers. Their owl-like faces feature large, piercing eyes and a sharp beak, ready to tear apart the soft flesh of its prey. No one knows if these strange beasts were created by nature or by magic, but everyone knows to steer clear when they're on the prowl.

Emerging at night, owlbears hunt alone or in mated pairs, scouring around their lair for fresh food. They are intelligent enough to know their hunting grounds, using their awful screeches and hoots to drive prey into areas from which there is no escape.

Owlbears are difficult to control, although with enough food, time, and luck, they can be trained to perform basic tasks. Goblins sometimes employ them as war mounts, while hill and frost giants favor them as pets. Even tamed, these creatures are unpredictable and dangerous, quick to turn on their masters if food runs low.

LAIR Owlbears make their dens in caves or ruins littered with the bones of their prey. These foul lairs give off the stench of blood and death, attracting other predators to the area. Their nocturnal hunting patterns mean their dens may be left empty during the darkest hours of the night.

DO THIS

Use bait to distract their attacks. Creatures this big need a lot of food to feel full. If your party wants to avoid a fight, try distracting the owlbear with fresh meat placed nearby.

Watch out for other enemies. While many owlbears are solitary beasts, others may have a mate—or even some cubs—nearby. The loud screeching of an owlbear in battle is sure to draw the interest of other predators in the area.

DON'T DO THIS

Don't think you can scare them away. Owlbears are intelligent, but not smart enough to know when they're in a losing battle. Spellcaster illusions, no matter how impressive, won't be enough to stop this fight once it begins.

Don't poke around an empty lair for too long. These nocturnal predators know their hunting grounds well. Their keen sight and smell will inform them of an intrusion to their den even from miles away.

SPRITE

POISONS AND POTIONS

Sprites are experts at turning plants and flowers into poisons or potions that can hurt, burn, or sometimes heal. Their favorite elixir is a sleeping drink that they dab onto their arrows. The arrows are tiny, but the potion is strong enough to take down a full-size adventurer.

SIZE Sprites grow to just over a foot tall, which makes them slightly taller than an average full-grown house cat. (And they're often just as needy!)

When imagining the tiny, winged woodland creatures known as sprites, you might picture adorable flower fairies from children's picture books—but don't be fooled. Sprites are warriors, through and through.

Despite their small size, sprites are a tough and serious-minded race of fighters who protect the woods and forests from trespassers. They're excellent judges of character, and if you enter their land with bad intentions they will not hesitate to take you down. On the other hand, if you come seeking their aid for a righteous cause, you may just get it.

Sprites are not a lot of fun to be around, unless you're really into fighting. They don't value art or creativity at all, unless it's the art of war and creating new types of poison to put on the tips of their arrows. (They *really* love poison arrows.)

Sprites are experts at camouflage, and can sneak through the underbrush without being heard. If they really want to stay hidden, sprites can also turn invisible, but that only lasts until they attack.

LAIR Sprite villages look like human villages, except smaller. They may be built into tree branches or roots, or under a canopy of vines, with mushroom roofs and bamboo walls. Sprite villages are defended vigilantly by patrols.

DO THIS

Tread carefully through the forest. If you accidentally squash a sprite, their vengeance is merciless.

Have magical healing at the ready. If your party doesn't have a cleric, paladin, or druid to provide healing spells, then stock up on anti-poison potions before you enter sprite territory.

DON'T DO THIS

Don't go looking for their villages. They'll see you before you see them.

Don't think small means weak. Sprites may be tiny, but every inch is packed with fighting spirit.

TREANT

SPECIAL POWERS

A treant is never alone in a forest. If you ever go up against one treant, you'll discover that they can temporarily bring two other trees to life to work or fight alongside them. You might find yourself surrounded, without even knowing which trees you're fighting!

LAIR
Treants live deep in wild forests, where they blend perfectly into their surroundings. Like ordinary trees, they live on sun, soil, and water, and they do not have any special or magical needs. Because treants are born from magic, their surroundings are often enchanted, and other magical beings may make their homes nearby.

SIZE
Treants can grow as large as any tree. That means there could be a treant up to three hundred feet tall! Because they take so long to awaken, you're unlikely to find a small treant. Even a modestly sized one will be at least twice the height of a logging truck, so you know who'd win in that face-off!

If a tree ever falls in the forest, there are always other trees to hear it. And some may even mourn it.

Very old trees growing in sacred or magical spaces can sometimes gain a spark of consciousness. They contemplate their place in the world for a very long time, and when the time is right, they awaken... and move.

These awakened trees are called treants, and they are large and mighty beings. As they slowly come to life, treants develop humanoid features, including legs and arms created from their roots and branches, and wizened faces of bark and knots in their trunks. In their early years, they are often protected by older treants or by other guardians of the forest.

Upon maturity, they become protectors of the forest, sensitive to everything that happens around them. They use their great strength to defend the magic and wonder of nature—and to punish any who transgress. Few things can hit as hard as a fist of hardened oak!

Though treants can stand and move, they rarely travel far. They prefer a peaceful life of contemplation, enjoying the tranquility of nature while reflecting on the mysteries of existence.

DO THIS

Let druids and rangers take the lead. These nature-loving classes are the best equipped to approach a treant without giving it offense.

Regard every tree as if it could be a treant. When a treant is at rest, it looks exactly like other trees.

Keep your fire-starter handy! If you ever have to keep an angry treant at bay, the threat of fire is very effective.

DON'T DO THIS

Don't disrespect the forest. Hurting healthy trees is the fastest way to anger a treant.

Don't get lost in enemy territory. Trying to hide from treants in trees is never a good idea.

Don't start forest fires. Threats may hold them back, but a treant will move to attack if they see real flames within their woods.

UNICORN

SPECIAL POWERS

Unicorns have several magical abilities, including the power to generate a protective field of shimmering energy, the ability to teleport up to a mile, and the power to heal the sick with the touch of its horn. Unicorns can also attack with their horns or their hooves, delivering magical damage.

SIZE Unicorns come in the same range of heights and sizes as ordinary horses. The unicorn's horn is the same length as an adult human forearm. These horns are known for their ability to channel magic. They can be ground up in potions or wielded like a wand. Forces of good will seek to punish anyone who uses a unicorn's horn in this way.

Unicorns look like horses with individual spiraling ivory horns, but they are actually something much stranger—celestial avatars of goodness that have come to the physical world from ethereal planes to protect sacred woodland spaces. Unicorns live in magic-rich forests, where they defend the innocent and vulnerable and try to keep the forces of evil at bay.

Attuned to nature, unicorns sense every sound and movement in the trees and bushes around them. They are also highly sensitive to virtue and can sense how good or bad a person is. They will gladly punish the unworthy (perhaps by skewering them with their horn), but they may also come to the aid of the worthy (usually by healing them of sickness or injury).

The most virtuous may even be allowed to ride a unicorn into battle against forces of great darkness, but this is very rare.

LAIR There are few places more beautiful than a unicorn's lair. Unicorns are so magical that their homes change to reflect their nature, resulting in peaceful glades and picture-perfect woodland scenes. In a unicorn's domain, birds sing more clearly and flowers seem to glow.

Other magical creatures are drawn to this sanctuary, where they are welcome under the unicorn's protection so long as they conduct themselves with virtue.

DO THIS

Approach with caution. If unicorns judge you unworthy to be in their presence, they'll let you know in a hurry.

Respect the unicorn's domain. Even a lifetime of good deeds won't help you if you try to steal magic from a unicorn.

DON'T DO THIS

Don't bring your hatred, jealousy, or evil into their domain. Unicorns will not tolerate any but the pure of heart within their sanctuary.

Don't seek power by using a unicorn's horn. They may be magical items, but they're not strong enough to protect you from the celestial forces that will seek revenge for your desecration.

UNICORN

As Kalista ventured deep into the forest, she could hear the fairy folk whispering and giggling. What could a creature like her ever want in a place like this? She flinched at every movement in the trees, yet she kept herself centered and calm. She had come to find an answer to a question, and she would not be turned away.

At last, she came to the clearing, a shallow pool of crystal-clear water nestled beneath silvery trees bursting with colorful blossoms, where she saw what she had come for. A unicorn drank from the pool, its magical horn seeming to shimmer in the midday light.

Kalista lived her whole life believing she was a monster. Born with obvious marks of her infernal tiefling heritage in a village that had never seen anything like her, she was told she carried darkness inside her and that her gifts of magic came from somewhere evil. The people she loved said that she was wicked and chased her from her home.

Yet she did not feel wicked in her heart.

Kalista was told unicorns could sense darkness in a person and would chase evil away from their sacred groves. She came to the forest to discover what the unicorn saw in her.

As she knelt near the noble creature, it looked up at her only briefly, and then returned its attention to the waters. The unicorn was not disturbed by her. It was not afraid. It was not threatened.

A tear ran down Kalista's cheek, for now she knew her heart had not lied.

Many would not have the courage to test themselves in such a way. If you ventured into an enchanted forest, how would the unicorn greet you?

GIANTS

Long before the empires of man, there were other kingdoms across these lands—the empires of the giants! These proud, titanic people were almost unopposed in their dominance of the world—except by the dragons, who would become their enduring foes.

Tales are still told of the epic wars between giants and dragons, which helped push both empires into decline. Today, giants live in remote and scattered clans, divided into six major races: hill giants, stone giants, frost giants, fire giants, cloud giants, and storm giants. All the races of giants have their own ideas about social standing that they call the *ordning*, which means "order." Storm giants look down on cloud giants, who look down on fire giants, who look down on frost giants, who look down on stone giants, who look down on hill giants. Hill giants aren't smart enough to know they're at the bottom, or smart enough to care. Each race also has their own way of figuring out rank within their own society, such as by wealth, strength, or even artistic talent. In hill giant society, your height and the size of your belly determine your social rank. They think bigger is always better!

Giants still cling to dreams of glory, and retain the physical strength and power to crush unwary travelers who cross their paths. If you ever happen across a giant, just hope that you're small enough to pass by unnoticed. That is, unless you think you're tough enough to take down a giant....

HILL GIANT

SIZE Even an average-size hill giant is taller than the largest African elephant— and probably a lot heavier too.

Of all the races of giants, hill giants are the ones you're most likely to run into on a very bad day. Heavy, dirty, stinky, and *mean*, they wander hills and valleys, plundering farms and homesteads for something to eat. Feeding their incredible appetites is really the only thing they care about, and you don't want to find yourself on the menu.

Hill giants look a lot like humans, but bigger and uglier, with a smell your nose might pick up from half a mile away. You'll likely find them dressed in ragged skins speckled with mud and brandishing a jagged old tree stump as a club. If you do see one, run away, because their attitude is just as nasty as their stench.

Nursery rhymes tell us that giants want to grind your bones to make their bread, but baking is probably a bit beyond a hill giant's skills, and it's definitely beyond their needs. They're more likely to eat you raw, in a few quick bites. They'll eat just about anything they can swallow, and they can swallow ... just about anything.

LAIR Hill giants live in mud huts or simple wooden shacks on hillsides and in valleys. Sometimes they try to take over the settlements of other races that they've chased away or devoured, but they're so big that they tend to accidentally destroy the buildings instead.

DO THIS	DON'T DO THIS
Sniff the air. If there's a hill giant nearby, you might smell them before you see them.	**Don't try to reason with a hill giant.** They're very bad at conversation.
Try to trick or hide from them. Because they're not very smart, hill giants are easy to deceive.	**Don't mistake any other type of giant for a hill giant.** They will take great offence at the comparison.
	Don't be too delicious!

STONE GIANT

2

READING THE RUNES Stone giants have developed a complex set of symbols they use to communicate stories and enchant magical items. They have great skill at carving rock and believe that studying carvings and runes can reveal the mysteries of the world. Prophecies are very popular among stone giants, and they might be persuaded to share some of their visions of the future with a thoughtful enough guest.

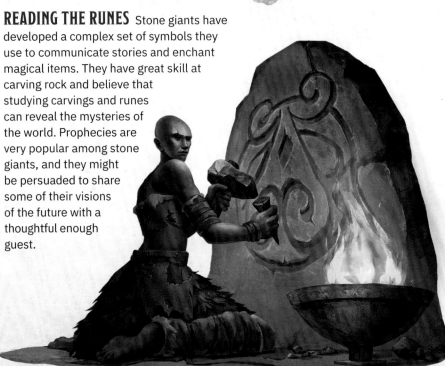

LAIR Stone giants love the dark and cold of the world far below our feet. Their elaborate networks of caves extend for miles. You can often identify these caves by the beautiful carved markings on the walls. Stone giants may live in communities, but they value peace and quiet so much that many also prefer to live alone.

SIZE At an average height of eighteen feet, stone giants are about as tall as one of those dancing tube figures that you might see outside a car dealership (though a stone giant probably wouldn't be very impressed if they met one).

Though stone giants rank just above hill giants (see page 40) in the social order, they are more civilized than their unruly cousins. They're not driven entirely by physical hunger, leaving them time to appreciate more complex concerns such as craft, contemplation, and solitude. Stone giants enjoy peace and quiet so much that the darker and quieter a place is, the more sacred they believe it to be. They're perfectly happy staying underground.

Because they live their lives almost entirely in caverns deep beneath the ground, stone giants have skin untouched by the sun and are almost as gray as the rocks that surround them. Get them above ground, however, and stone giants can be very dangerous. They regard the surface as a sort of dream world where nothing is real, and where their actions don't have consequences. The farther they are from home, the more trouble they can cause.

Stone giant society is ranked according to refinement and skill, whether it's the excellence of their artistry or their grace as athletes. Those who lack such talents are often relegated to the fringes of their community, serving as guards and hunters for their more sophisticated cousins.

DO THIS

Watch the walls. Stone giants can camouflage themselves against rock and stone.

Admire their work. Stone giants work hard on their craft, and they may respond well to flattery.

Meet them underground. The closer a stone giant is to the surface, the more violent they're likely to be.

DON'T DO THIS

Don't run. A stone giant can throw rocks far and with tremendous accuracy. If you're not careful, you could get squished before you reach safety.

Don't lose your way. If you venture into the caverns and cross paths with a stone giant, you'll want to remember the quickest way back to the surface.

FROST GIANT

TROPHIES Because frost giants love war, they also love trophies, whether taken from the settlements they've destroyed or made from the bodies of the enemies they've slain. That might include a majestic weapon or a jewel so huge that only a giant can wear it. But there's nothing a frost giant loves more than a trophy that shows they've bested a dragon.

If you're crossing the frozen wastelands and hear the wail of a war horn through the swirl of the frigid winds, it's probably already too late for you to run and seek shelter. The frost giants are coming.

Frost giants are weather-hardened warriors who make their homes in lands of ice and snow, where very little grows and even less survives. Their skin is blue and cold to the touch, and their hair is white and crusted with ice. They avoid the sun and shun fire. There is no room for warmth in a frost giant's life.

Because they live in such barren territory, frost giants raid and pillage for food and goods. As a result, their entire society is built around war and strength. In fact, the social order among frost giants is based on how tough you are, whether it's the size of your muscles or the number of scars you have. Frost giants are more than happy to test their strength against each other to see who comes out on top.

LAIR Frost giants reside in cold and desolate places, in ice-rimed glacial caves or on the highest snow-capped mountains. You're much more likely to encounter a frost giant on one of their raids into neighboring territory, but if you do ever stumble upon a frost giant's lair, don't expect a warm welcome.

SIZE Frost giants are slightly taller than the tallest giraffe, though the chances of a frost giant ever encountering a giraffe are slim.

DO THIS	DON'T DO THIS
Stay in the sun. Frost giants don't venture too far from home, and you'll never come across them in a warm climate.	**Don't show any weakness.** Frost giants only respect strength.
Listen for the war horn. If you're ever in territory that's close to a frost giant's lair, have your escape route planned in case you hear their war horn blare.	**Don't go into frozen wastelands.** At least not without a good dog pack or trusty steed to carry you swiftly out again.

FROST GIANT

Bruenor clung to the protected side of a snowy outcropping as his keen eyes scanned the mountain for movement. Wind whipped swirls of snow into the air, making it hard to judge distance or see imminent threats. After decades traversing the north, enduring some of the harshest weather imaginable in all of Faerûn, the dwarven warrior was used to the cold, but it didn't make his job any easier.

Just as Bruenor's mind started to wander with thoughts of cracking open his rations to have a snack, he saw his target: a frost giant, towering above the trees, marching along the mountain as easily as a human or dwarf would traverse a hiking trail. From Bruenor's hidden vantage point, the giant's head was almost level. He could see that its battered helmet and ring-mail armor spoke of many battles fought and won. Slung on its back was a double-headed axe large enough to chop a house in half.

The dwarf had an axe of his own, notched by dozens of brutal battles. The weapon had served him well over the years. If Bruenor charged now and jumped, he might be able to surprise the giant and wound it, giving him the advantage in combat. If he stayed hidden, he'd be safe, but then the giant would almost certainly attack the nearby village, once it saw smoke from the fires down below. Could the dwarf sneak away and warn them without being seen? Should he make a lot of noise and distract the giant instead?

Whatever he was going to do, he had to decide *now*.

What happens next? Does Bruenor attack the frost giant, using his mighty axe against his opponent—and if he does, is the weapon sharp enough to pierce the giant's thick hide? Does he remain hidden, thinking up a plan that will use his wits as well as his weapon to save the village? It's up to you!

FIRE GIANT

MASTERS OF THE FORGE

Fire giants are talented blacksmiths who excel at making armor, iron fortifications, and the deadliest and heaviest weapons, some of which are huge even by a giant's standards. However, as beautiful and well-crafted as their weapons can be, fire giants also share all giants' fondness for just hurling really big rocks.

SIZE Fire giants grow to an average height of about eighteen feet, which means they're about the right height to look through the upper window of a two-story house (if this happens to you, run for the fire escape)!

With skin as dark as ash and hair as bright as flame, everything about the fire giant reminds you of their obsession with fire. Their ornate armor and terrifying weapons should give you a clue about their other obsession: war.

Fire giants live in a militaristic society that prizes valor, conquest, and battle tactics. Fire giants train as soldiers their entire lives, and their social order is determined by both strength and intelligence (because winning a war is never *just* about might). Fire giants are highly competitive and many of their leaders are determined to advance their rank in the great ordning.

Blacksmiths are also held in high regard in fire giant society, as the blacksmith's forge is the heart of the fire giant war machine. Fire giants appreciate craft and skill, and their blacksmiths always work to improve their weapons and invent new ones to meet any challenge.

LAIR If you've ever wanted to visit a lair built inside a volcano, venture forth in search of the fire giants. They build incredible fortress castles underground, ideally on top of bubbling molten lava pits. If there isn't a volcano nearby, expect to find them mining for coal or destroying forests to fuel their enormous forges.

DO THIS

Stay cool. Fire giants don't like to venture far from a heat source.

Learn a song. Fire giants love war songs, so you might win their favor by appealing to their vanity and singing about their great victories. This is where your party's bard can really shine.

DON'T DO THIS

Don't underestimate them. Fire giants value strength, but also intelligence. They're not simple brutes like hill giants.

Don't get caught. Fire giants put their prisoners to work in the mines. So if they capture you, you might never escape.

DUKE ZALTO

💀
5

Like all fire giants, an average person would stand somewhere between Zalto's knee and his belt as he towers overhead. His arm is thicker than your whole body and each of his fingers are wider than your whole head.

Duke Zalto is a fire giant warlord with an obsession. Zalto believes he can become ruler of all giants by building an ancient war colossus called the Vonindod. An angry eighteen-foot-tall warrior with an even more gigantic monster machine? Yeah, it's a scary possibility and someone needs to stop him.

Even without the Vonindod, Zalto is tougher than the average fire giant. He's an experienced soldier who has fought in dozens of battles. He carries a massive *maul* (a war hammer wielded with two hands) that's so big he can keep a human-size prisoner in the cage on top, and he has two huge dogs (named Narthor and Zerebor) that follow him wherever he goes.

LAIR Zalto lives in Ironslag, a gargantuan stronghold embedded in Mount Hamarhaast, north of the Silver Marches. Standing at five hundred feet high, Ironslag is a multilevel fortress with twisting mines, a forge, and a prison. Entering Ironslag requires figuring out how to get past fifty-foot-tall adamantine doors sealed with ancient magic. Even if you do make your way inside, you'll have to contend with goblins, ogres, chimera, and the many fire giants loyal to the Duke before confronting Zalto himself.

ZALTO'S FAMILY Zalto is dangerous, and he's not alone. While exploring Ironslag, you may meet members of his family as well.

  Brimskarda: Zalto's wife, an angry fire giant woman annoyed with her husband's desire to build the Vonindod.

  Cinderhild: Zalto's daughter, a frustrated fire giant teen who wishes she could leave Ironslag and explore the world outside.

  Zaltember: Zalto's son, a lazy and cruel fire giant teen who enjoys hurting smaller creatures for fun.

THE VONINDOD The Vonindod, also known as the Titan of Death, is an ancient construct that Zalto hopes to rebuild in order to raise his ranking within the giants' ordning.

If completed, the colossus will stand eighty feet tall with eyes made from giant rubies and armor of invulnerable adamantine. Four times the size of a fire giant, the Vonindod could wrestle an ancient dragon to the ground or punch a hole in a mountain with its huge metal hands. Zalto must be stopped before he brings the Vonindod back to life!

CLOUD GIANT

SPECIAL POWERS Cloud giants often use magic to control the weather—to summon clouds or fog, to carry themselves on the wind or move objects around, or even to call down lightning to destroy a foe. All cloud giants share the ability to transform themselves into foggy mist and to walk on clouds.

SIZE Cloud giants are the second-largest race of giants, averaging about twenty-four feet tall. That means they're about the height of four tall men standing on each other's shoulders.

If you've ever dreamed of climbing a beanstalk all the way up to the clouds and then venturing into a giant's home to steal their great treasures, the cloud giants would like to have a word with you. Because those are *their* treasures, and they don't want to share.

Pale, athletic, and distinguished, cloud giants live in a society defined by wealth and beauty. They dress in finery, adorn themselves with exotic jewels, and surround themselves with lavish treasures and wonderful works of art. Rank in cloud giant society is determined by wealth and by the beauty and generosity of one's gifts.

An elite race, cloud giants consider the world below to be a trivial place, only valuable as a source of more treasure or entertainment. They sometimes place bets on the outcomes of mortal wars. (Indeed, one of the only times they might interfere in the affairs of lesser races is when the wager isn't going their way.)

LAIR Cloud giants take pride in the beauty of their homes, so they would prefer that you *not* refer to them as "lairs." They live in palaces and castles, either high on mountaintops or up in the clouds themselves, which are surrounded by extravagant gardens of giant-size fruits and bright blooming flowers.

DO THIS

Show respect. Cloud giants can be very vain, and they appreciate flattery.

Watch out for their pets! Instead of keeping cats or dogs as pets, cloud giants keep griffons, giant eagles, or flying tigers.

Challenge them to a game. Cloud giants can't resist a challenge. If a cloud giant has you cornered, a game of chance may be your **only** hope of escape.

DON'T DO THIS

Don't steal. Proud of their homes and their treasures, cloud giants **won't** forget if you take something from them.

Don't hide. Cloud giants can sniff you out wherever you hide.

Definitely don't hide in the mist. Sometimes the mist **is** the cloud giant.

STORM GIANT

SPECIAL POWERS Just as the name suggests, storm giants are masters of the storm. Their innate magical abilities not only allow them to control weather (like their cloud giant cousins on page 52), but also to hurl lightning bolts directly from their hands. Storm giants also have the gift of prophecy. By reading patterns and omens, they can foretell the rise and fall of empires.

LAIR Storm giant lairs have one thing in common: they are almost impossible to reach. Whether storm giants choose to make their home on a remote mountain, in the deepest and darkest trench of an ocean, or so high up in the clouds that they can almost touch the stars, storm giants keep their distance. They don't even spend much time around each other and don't expect many visitors.

SIZE Storm giants are the biggest of all the giant races, and they grow to an average height of about twenty-six feet. That makes them about ten feet taller than a famous London double-decker bus.

Pale and elegant, storm giants are largely peaceful beings despite their terrifying size and tremendous power. They live for hundreds of years and have long memories, so most are happy watching history go by, waiting for the day when their kingdom grows strong again and they can rule the world once more.

Storm giants are typically distant and aloof. When they do sometimes bother to involve themselves in the affairs of smaller, more short-lived creatures though, they can bring an entire country to its knees. As you've already probably figured out, it's usually better to leave storm giants alone.

Even still, if you're looking for some advice, a visit to a storm giant can be very rewarding. They can see the past and catch glimpses of possible futures. Come to them with proper respect and a good heart, and they may be willing to help you.

Storm giants are above all other giants in rank, and they do not care about the power struggles of the giants beneath them. Among their own kind they rarely battle for status, preferring to live secluded lives of contemplation if possible.

DO THIS

Keep your distance. You could comfortably go your whole life without ever meeting a storm giant.

Show proper respect. Storm giants are wise and ancient. They're used to being treated like gods. If you disrespect them, they may destroy you . . . **and** everyone around you.

DON'T DO THIS

Don't impose on a storm giant. They enjoy their own company, not yours!

Don't try to trick them. Very little escapes storm giants' notice, and they have no time for fools.

MOORS, BOGS & BONEYARDS

The dead do not always rest peacefully. Graveyards may be filled with evil energy and dark creatures who are ready to strike out in envy against the living.

Nor are graveyards always where you think. The churchyard dotted with stone markers is obvious, but an open field may be the resting place of ancient warriors felled in a great battle, or a dark cave may mark where an orc tribe once disposed of their dead.

Boneyards are not alone in harboring dark energies. Windswept moors and swampy bogs are steeped in solitude and despair, a perfect domain for the restless undead.

Regardless of where you find them, these places contain both deadly forces and hidden treasures for the adventurer brave enough to challenge their dangers. Are you ready to face what lives outside life itself?

TURNING THE UNDEAD

The undead are unholy creatures existing in a state no longer living but also not quite deceased. For this reason, holy power wielded by the faithful can force undead monsters to turn away, flee, or, in some extreme cases, even explode on the spot. Cleric or paladins of certain faiths have access to this turning power, and it can be quite a potent tool when battling creatures risen from the dead.

BANSHEE

SPECIAL POWERS

HORRIFYING VISAGE
By distorting their terrifying faces, the banshee can render their opponents immobile with fear!

DETECTION OF LIFE
Banshees are drawn to the energy of living creatures, whose presence can be sensed up to five miles away.

INCORPOREAL MOVEMENT
Banshees can move through objects and other creatures with mild difficulty. Doors and walls won't stop them!

WAIL
Once per night, a banshee can unleash a horrifying scream that causes physical damage to any living creature within range.

Across the darkness of the night, a terrible wail sounds, sending fear shivering down the spine of even the bravest warrior. It is the call of the banshee, the corrupted spirit of a female elf. These cursed creatures misused their great beauty in life and are now condemned to suffer for their cruelty in death.

Banshees feel no joy or happiness, only pain at the presence of living creatures who remind them of all they have lost. They hoard beautiful treasures, surrounding themselves with art, jewels, and other objects reflecting their vanity in life. They mourn for their own lost loveliness, and a single glance in a mirror will drive one into a murderous rage. Few are prepared to face a banshee's full wrath!

LAIR Banshees are bound to the place of their death and cannot travel more than five miles from that spot. Many died in once-luxurious mansions, now crumbling to dust, and others expired in the wilderness, having driven away everyone who cared for them in life.

SIZE As the spirit of a female elf, banshees retain roughly the same shape and size in death. Their forms are luminous and wispy, surrounded by a tangle of wild hair and tattered rags that float around them in a ghostly manner.

DO THIS	DON'T DO THIS
Fight from a distance. The banshee's touch carries a necrotic energy that does damage to living creatures.	**Don't show off your treasures.** Banshees covet beautiful objects and will stop at nothing to add your shiny things to their collections.
Use magical weapons and attack spells. Banshees are resistant to all types of damage from normal weapons, so now's the time to break out that magic sword or fireball spell.	**Don't count on walls, gates, or other obstacles to protect you.** A banshee can phase right through such objects to reach her target.

SKELETON

PAST LIVES Skeletons have no conscious memory of their past selves, but many retain habits from their former lives. These habits sometimes emerge when a skeleton is left without specific orders to follow. For instance, a skeleton of a farmer might start hoeing the ground, or the skeletons of nobles might carry out an eternal dance in an abandoned ballroom.

Lacking memory of language, skeletons cannot speak, so they communicate only with basic gestures.

SIZE A skeleton's size changes based on the bones used to create it. While standard races such as humans and elves are most common, powerful mages have managed to revive the bones of huge creatures, like dragons and giants—not to mention cobbling together unique creations from a mix of different bones!

Animated by dark magic, skeletons are bony warriors summoned forth by spellcasters or who arise of their own accord from graves steeped in necromantic energy and ancient evils. In whatever fashion they are created, these relentless foes fight without mercy and attack until destroyed—for the evil energy that made them also drives them to kill all living creatures.

Obedient servants, skeletons are capable of complex tasks, like firing a catapult or dropping boiling oil on enemies below, provided each step is carefully explained. They move and fight in a simple manner, pursuing their goals with mindless determination, and make excellent guards.

While most skeletons are humanoid, bones of all types can be brought back to life with powerful enough magic, and adventurers may find themselves facing down all manner of strange and deadly skeletal forms!

LAIR Skeletons may be found in the graveyards or ancient battlegrounds where their bones once laid at rest. They can also be found guarding castles and estates for necromancers and other powerful sorcerers.

DO THIS

Fight like your life depends on it. Skeletons never give up, so you can't either!

Take advantage of obstacles. Skeletons' limited mental capacity means they are easily slowed by doors, furniture, and other hindrances.

Call upon your party's clerics. Divine magic allows clerics to turn the undead, the only power that can stop a skeleton's relentless attacks.

DON'T DO THIS

Don't try to reason with them. They won't be swayed, no matter how charismatic you are.

Don't underestimate how they'll attack. Most skeletons fight in a simple, straightforward manner, but they're capable of complex battle moves if orders are given carefully enough.

SKELETON

It was an easy gig. That's what the thieves' guild had promised Shandie when she took the assignment. Ride in, grab the goblet, ride back out.

Nobody mentioned the curse, or the skeletons that came with it.

Shandie had seen the green light when she lifted the goblet from its pedestal, and had felt the flow of some malevolent energy rattle across her fingertips before it dispersed into the night. There had been silence for a moment, broken only by the sound of wind through the spruce trees outside and the buzz of a persistent mosquito that'd been tailing her since her last river crossing. Then there came a dreadful grinding, like old bones being rubbed together, and the damp thump of moving dirt.

The halfling whirled around, unsheathing her trusty short sword. One skeleton she could handle, but she'd spotted a graveyard on her way in. Who knows how many of these things would be summoned by the curse? Shandie considered putting the goblet back where she'd found it, which might be enough to calm them down and disperse the evil magic that summoned them. Then again, the payout for this job was pretty sweet. Maybe she could fight her way through them all . . . if she was fast enough. She weighed the goblet in one hand and her sword in the other, trying to make a choice in the scant seconds left before the skeleton attacked.

What should Shandie do next? If she does defeat the skeleton in front of her, how many more will be waiting outside? If she puts the goblet back in its place, will that be enough to break the spell? Can she find a way to escape that uses her wits and speed more than her sword? It's up to you!

VAMPIRES

Vampires are the risen dead, hungering for the life they have lost—a yearning only satisfied by drinking the blood of the living! Undeath twists what few emotions vampires retain: love becomes sick obsession; friendship warps to bitter jealousy. They replace feelings with physical objects that stand in for lost emotions, collecting art and treasures that soothe—momentarily— their eternal emptiness.

Lands infested by one of these creatures see an increase in the numbers of vermin. Plants wither, or grow in twisted knots, while shadows move of their own accord and a creeping fog clings to the earth. Only slaying the vampire can lift the blight.

Vampire spawn are created when a vampire feeds on a living creature and allows its victim to expire without tasting the vampire's blood in return. The spawn gain some of the vampire's powers, including regeneration, which allows the monster to slowly restore its health during combat (unless it is unconscious), and spider climbing, which allows the creature to easily scale difficult surfaces, such as vertical walls and upside down on ceilings!

Although mighty, vampires and their spawn have their weaknesses. Sunlight burns them, and they cannot cross running water, such as a stream or river. Their curse prevents them from entering a home unless invited inside by a resident. Their forms cast neither shadows nor reflections, and many a mortal has been saved by noticing a missing reflection before the vampire's fangs find their throat. Finally, a wooden stake driven through their heart instantly paralyzes a vampire, leaving them vulnerable to death by decapitation.

VAMPIRE LORD

4

SPECIAL POWERS

CHARM

A living victim influenced by this power sees the vampire as a trusted friend, making them open to the creature's suggestions and willing to receive its bite!

SUMMONING

During the night, a vampire may call a horde of bats or rats to do their bidding; when outside, they can also command a pack of wolves in the same way!

SHAPESHIFTING

Vampires can transform into a bat, letting them fly while retaining all their mystical powers.

MIST

When injured, a vampire converts into a cloud of mist that flees toward its resting place. If a misted vampire reaches its coffin, it can regenerate its physical body!

SIZE Vampires are transformed humanoids and have the same size as a typical member of their mortal species.

Alone, a vampire is a formidable enemy. Clever and cunning, they may use charm to sway mortals to their service, or spy unseen in one of their shape-changing forms. They are fierce fighters, moving with alarming speed and delivering a deadly bite with their sharp fangs. Even when your weapons land solid blows, the vampire's ability to regenerate pulls victory further from your grasp!

But worse, these fearsome creatures surround themselves with loyal servants, both their own spawn and other undead, who protect their master at any cost. Vampires can exist forever, draining the blood of the living and infesting the surrounding lands with the aura of their evil presence. Their eternal scourge can only be ended by the courage and strength of a mighty adventurer!

LAIR Vampires choose majestic yet defendable lairs, often castles or manors. Their coffins are typically hidden in underground crypts or guarded vaults. They are forced to lie within their coffins during the day, but can move this location by transporting the coffin or a large amount of grave dirt to a new resting spot.

DO THIS

Call upon nature's power. Sunlight and running water are among the greatest weaknesses of a vampire, so find ways to bring those into your battle!

Bring along a holy spellcaster. If your party doesn't already have a cleric, now is a good time to ask the local churches if anyone is willing to join you on your quest. Their ability to turn the undead is crucial when fighting vampires.

DON'T DO THIS

Don't ignore the warning signs. If the locals are worried about an increase in rats or creepy mist that rolls in at sunset, a vampire may be taking up residence. Root it out before it can establish a formidable lair!

Don't forget to look up. A vampire's climbing powers mean it can attack from several directions, including overhead.

VAMPIRE SPAWN

💀
3

SPECIAL POWERS As creatures weaker than their makers, vampire spawn do not possess the full range of undead powers. They can call upon only regeneration and spider climb (see page 65). Vampire spawn may also use their claws and teeth for dangerous attacks!

SIZE Vampire spawn are transformed humanoids and have the same size as a typical member of their mortal species. However, their physical size does not always reflect the cursed strength they possess!

Vampire spawn are ravenous creatures under the control of their creator, loyal and obedient to all commands. They share the vampire's endless thirst, and seek out fresh victims whenever their master allows. Their lack of free will means they cannot access the most powerful of the vampire's abilities, but their feral cunning and relentless hunger have still been the downfall of many adventurers.

Some vampires create spawn specifically to function as servants or guards, devoted during the night and hiding in their coffins during the day. Other spawn may be used to prey upon the living residents of the vampire's realm, spreading fear and death wherever they go. Either way, the eternal loyalty of vampire spawn can only be broken by the death of their creator—which gives them back their free will.

LAIR You'll find vampire spawn within the grand castles and mansions of their vampire master. A rare few may haunt lonely graveyards or other remote sites, chained to their burial place by their undead curse.

DO THIS

Stock up on stakes. The paralysis wears off once the stake is removed, so you'll need one for every vampire spawn you're up against.

Keep a mirror near your front door. That way, you can be sure any strangers seeking help in the night have a reflection before you let them in.

DON'T DO THIS

Don't negotiate. The bond between a vampire spawn and its master is mystical in nature and cannot be broken, even by threats of death.

Don't delay in dealing with them. Once their master is killed, vampire spawn regain their free will—which means they may come after you looking for revenge.

COUNT STRAHD VON ZAROVICH

SPECIAL POWERS As if being a vampire wasn't enough, Strahd has used his centuries of existence to hone his magical abilities. He can cast a wide range of spells, including ones to detect thoughts, animate the dead, create illusions, and even throw fireballs.

In life, Count Strahd was a prince, a soldier, a conqueror, and a student of dark magics. Hundreds of years into his vampiric reign over Barovia, a vast valley filled with dark forests and surrounded by looming mountains, he is all this and more, a terrifying creature of remorseless evil and cold brilliance. Detached from all human emotion, Strahd takes joy in the conquest of mortal souls, corrupting where he can and destroying where he cannot. His vampire powers are enhanced by powerful spellcasting, including the ability to animate the dead!

The doors of Ravenloft Castle, Strahd's realm, are always unlocked; those who enter must prepare themselves to face a remorseless enemy who delights in testing his opponents with both brute force and treachery. Is your party up to the task?

LAIR Count Strahd dwells within the mighty castle of Ravenloft, an opulent gothic structure protected by hordes of undead creatures. His mystical connection with his lair allows him to pass through its walls without resistance or open and lock doors with just a thought. Strahd's evil influence has spread eternal night not only over the castle but across the entire land of Barovia—a darkness only you can dispel by defeating the count himself.

STRAHD'S MINIONS To really fight Strahd, you'll need to get through the dangerous creatures who guard him first. Within the halls of Ravenloft, you'll find wolves and bats, ghosts and ghouls, even skeletons and vampire spawn.

HEART OF SORROW Hidden deep within the walls of Ravenloft is a giant crystal called the Heart of Sorrow. Any damage that Count Strahd takes during combat is magically transferred to this gem, allowing him to shrug off the mightiest of blows. You'll need to find and destroy this magical crystal before you can take Count Strahd down for good!

SIZE In his normal form, Count Strahd is a tall, muscular humanoid, clad in expensive robes and armor. His shapeshifting powers allow him to transform into a small bat, a medium-size wolf, and an untouchable cloud of mist.

OCEANS, LAKES & WATERWAYS

W ater is the source of life. We came from that primordial swirl, it sustains every growing thing around us, and we return to it all the time, to drink, to bathe, and to experience tranquility.

Don't be fooled. Water brings life, but it can also take it. There are plenty of creatures lurking beneath the waves that might wish you harm … and many of them have teeth!

Out in the depths, something great and terrible may be swimming toward an unsuspecting fisherman. Closer to the shoreline, an unwary explorer may cross an unseen boundary, entering the territory of a fierce and merciless foe. Even in lakes and rivers, a charming stranger could lure you to your doom.

If you thought it was safe to drink from a stream or soak in the sea, think again. Deadly creatures may be lurking just beneath the surface.

ABOLETH

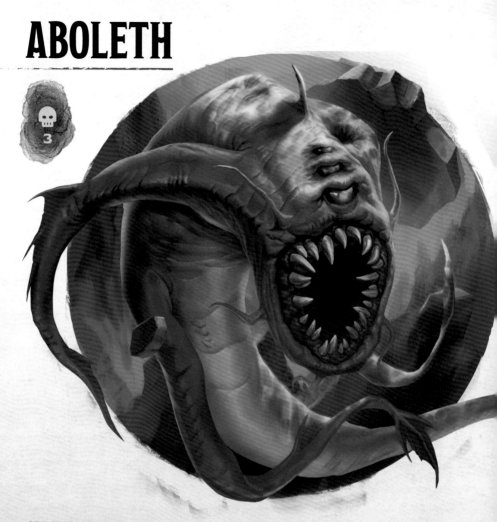

SPECIAL POWERS An aboleth can strike you with its tail or tentacles or contaminate you with its mucus; but that's not even the worst. Their psychic attacks allow them to enslave your mind, controlling your actions and draining your energy to heal itself.

SIZE Aboleths usually grow to about twenty feet in length, which makes them about a third bigger than a female great white shark. However, there are reports that some of the most ancient and powerful aboleths can grow to twice that size.

With eyes as dark as the deepest ocean, mouths with more deadly teeth than any shark, and long, writhing, powerful tentacles that exude toxic mucus, you may imagine that aboleths are some of the most terrifying predators under the sea. They *are*, and even worse than you can envision!

These huge and terrible creatures are the fallen masters of lost civilizations, and their most potent weapons are their minds. Aboleths have the power to psychically enslave mortal creatures, and they once abused this power to make people worship them, forcing the compelled masses to build temples in their honor.

The true gods took offense at this sacrilege and destroyed the aboleths' empire. The aboleths have lurked in darkness ever since, vowing to one day have their revenge.

Aboleths never forget an enemy. In fact, aboleths never forget anything. Even worse, aboleths never truly die, so if you ever destroy one, it will eventually come back ... and then it will come for you.

LAIR Ruins of ancient aboleth civilizations still survive to this day, deep in the dark recesses of the ocean or in flooded caverns far beneath our feet. Proud and bitter aboleths still swim among these ruins, where their magic is at its strongest. Aboleths can control the foul water flowing through their lairs and use it to drown unwary visitors or as a channel for their psychic rage.

DO THIS

Stay in the shallows. Steer clear of deep water that contains ancient ruins or clouds of mucus.

Guard your thoughts. Before you meet an aboleth, find a spell or artifact that can protect you against mind attacks.

DON'T DO THIS

Don't believe your eyes. Aboleths can get inside your head and cast illusions.

Don't trust anyone who tells you aboleths are okay. They're probably being mind-controlled.

DRAGON TURTLE

SPECIAL POWERS

AMPHIBIOUS
Dragon turtles can breathe both air and water, allowing them to move swiftly between environments.

BASHING ATTACK
With a single smash of their mighty tails, dragon turtles can knock their opponents off their feet and push them ten feet away, making it impossible to fight back.

STEAM BREATH
Dragon turtles can shoot out a sixty-foot blast of boiling-hot steam that injures everyone in its path.

SIZE An adult dragon turtle is between thirty-five and sixty feet long and can weigh up to 250,000 pounds. That's about the size of an old-fashioned sailing ship, and the same weight as a space shuttle.

Dragon turtles are among the most fearsome of all ocean dwellers, capable of taking down ships with their crushing jaws, steaming breath, and smashing tails. Their enormous shells are a deep green color, the same shade as the ocean depths where they reside. Silver patterns on their shells mimic light bouncing off the waves, making them hard to spot by even the most diligent lookout.

Although not true dragons (see page 87), these creatures share their namesake's love of treasure. Clever sailors will bribe dragon turtles with jewels and other glittering goodies in exchange for safe passage through watery realms. Unlucky mariners will find their ship capsized by an attack, during which the dragon turtle swallows all the treasure it can find for transport back to its underwater cave.

LAIR Dragon turtles live in caves hidden among coral reefs, below the sea floor, or along a rugged coastline. Their lairs glitter with stolen treasure, and they tolerate no intruders.

DO THIS

Keep watch from the crow's nest. Dragon turtles may attack day or night. Watch for unnatural patterns of light on the water—that may mean a dragon turtle is close at hand.

Be ready to bribe them. Your party might decide that a shiny bauble is less valuable than safe passage through a dragon turtle's domain.

Find a crew who knows the dangers of the sea. Before you book passage, talk with the ship's crew to ensure they're prepared for the risks that might lie ahead.

DON'T DO THIS

Don't waste your arrows. A dragon turtle's thick shell is impenetrable to all but the mightiest of magics. If you must attack with non-magical weapons, aim for the softer underbelly.

Don't think that a life raft will save you. Abandoning ship won't be enough to save you from a dragon turtle, not if they think you've brought treasure with you on your escape.

MERROW

TOOTH AND CLAW The bite of a merrow can do a lot of damage, but the slash of its claws is even more dangerous. Here's the really bad news: a merrow will often attack with both teeth and claws at once.

SIZE Merrow grow to a length of about twelve feet, which is about as long as two terrified humans placed end to end as they desperately try to escape a merrow's grasp.

There are tribes of gentle merfolk living beneath the waves, peaceful communities that love to swim and play. The merrow are not those merfolk.

Legend says a tribe of merfolk fell under the curse of an ancient artifact that bound them to Demogorgon, a diabolical being also known as the Prince of Demons (see page 20). Ensnared by Demogorgon's madness, the merfolk's king conducted a ritual that opened a gateway to the Abyss, Demogorgon's dark dimension.

As a result, the merfolk were corrupted with madness and distorted into monstrous new forms, with sharklike teeth and terrible claws. They emerged from the Abyss as a new race of vicious predators who would attack ships, drown and devour sailors, and hoard treasures. They delight in spreading chaos and fear, which serves to feed the power of their demon lord.

LAIR If you ever find a string of corpses threaded together beneath the sea, beware; you are at the boundary of a merrow lair. This ghoulish display warns adventurers not to try their luck raiding the deep-sea caves of the merrow, which are often rich with plundered loot and sunken treasures.

DO THIS	DON'T DO THIS
Stay alert at the water's edge. Merrow can surge out of the sea in a flash.	**Don't stray into unknown waters alone.** You never know what dangers may lurk beneath, so be sure to bring backup.
Watch each other's backs in a merrow fight. Their skill at stealth means all members of your party need to protect one another or risk being hit with an unexpected attack.	**Don't play with strange artifacts.** If you don't know what something does, don't play with it—unless you want to wind up as cursed as the merrow.

MOUNTAIN PEAKS & OPEN SKY

In the skies above us, monsters make their homes at the top of mountains, soaring through the air or floating just out of reach. These flying creatures can assault their targets from above or swoop down and strike when least expected. The sky is their playground and they know how to use it to their advantage.

A battle in flight can be more dangerous than almost any other. Not only can attacks come from any side at any time, but losing means falling from incredible heights to crash down upon the ground. The denizens who make the air their home can be vicious against those who wish to visit their domain. Are you ready to fly?

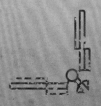

GRIFFON

RIDING A GRIFFON A fully grown wild griffon will never let you ride it and will likely tear you to pieces if you try.

However, if you find a griffon's egg and raise a griffon from a hatchling, you might be able to train it to be your loyal steed, and a griffon will serve you extremely well in battle. If you don't know *how* to train a griffon, it will probably tear you to pieces.

SIZE Though they have the body of a lion and the head and wings of an eagle, griffons are a little bigger than lions and a *lot* bigger than eagles. Even the most powerful stallion might be no match for a griffon's claws and beak.

A horse can be an adventurer's best friend when it comes to covering large distances in a short time and carrying plenty of weapons, supplies, or treasures with you. However, your best friend has its own worst enemy, as you'll discover if you ever ride your horse into griffon territory.

Griffons have the head, wings, and claws of an eagle, and the body and strength of a lion, all of which make them powerful and terrifying hunters. Their favorite prey? Horses. Griffons live in prides, like lions, and each pride is fiercely protective of its territory. Moving with the speed of an eagle, they can swoop down on you in a flash—and after they strike with the force of a lion, you may be finished off before you know what hit you. Of course, they're usually more interested in your horse than they are in you.

LAIR Griffons live on craggy mountains, where they build giant nests among the cracks and crevices. If you ever get a close look at a griffon's nest, you might notice that it's not just made of sticks and grass; it may also be made of the bones of their prey. Oh, and if you're that close to a griffon's nest, you're probably next on the menu.

DO THIS

Ride in disguise. Buy some camouflage for your horse before entering griffon territory to avoid attacks.

Jump off if a griffon grabs your horse. The beast will hold on to its prey and let you escape.

DON'T DO THIS

Don't rush in at full gallop. You hear clattering hooves, but a griffon hears the ringing of a dinner bell.

Don't steal their eggs! The idea of a raised-from-birth griffon mount sounds great now, but it won't be as much fun when mamma griffon comes after her baby.

Don't mistake a griffon's cry for an eagle's. The griffon's cry is much deeper and louder—and getting it wrong could be deadly!

PEGASUS

RIDING A PEGASUS

Pegasi are as intelligent as many humanoid races, which means they can't be broken and tamed like ordinary horses. The only way you'll get to ride a pegasus is if they let you, which means building a bond of trust first. Pegasi have a strong sense of right and wrong, and they'll only trust you if they sense that you're a good person.

SIZE Pegasi come in the same variety of sizes as regular horses, but with one big difference—wings. Pegasus wings can extend to a span of about twenty feet, which is about the width of a townhouse!

The wild and wondrous pegasus is a rare sight for any adventurer to behold. While ordinary horses are an everyday encounter for many, you could live a hundred years and never see a single one of these winged wonders, both because pegasi are so uncommon and because they prefer to keep their distance from others.

According to legend, pegasi originate from another plane of reality, a realm of stunning beauty protected by elflike beings. The rulers of this realm ride the flying beasts as their steeds. Sometimes pegasi travel through into the ordinary world, perhaps to come to the aid of those who truly need their help.

Pegasi retain the wild nature and otherworldly majesty of their home realm. All pegasi are white as snow, but their wings and their coloration are not the only things that mark them apart from ordinary horses. They're also much smarter, which is why they keep their distance from the dangerous worlds of men and monsters.

LAIR Pegasi spend most of their time in the air, their wings never tiring. They typically only set down on the ground to eat or drink. When they do so, it's often in remote locations where there's no one else around.

DO THIS	DON'T DO THIS
Approach slowly and with respect. These clever creatures are quick to flee from those they do not trust.	**Don't try to tame a pegasus.** They will resist.
Treat pegasi as your equals. They're as smart as any human and will not tolerate being treated as simple beasts of the field.	**Don't try to sneak up on them.** They will fly away in a hurry.
	Don't feed them too many sugar cubes. Sugar is bad for their teeth—and for yours!

DRAGONS

In worlds of fantasy and adventure, stories are told about the most famous of magical creatures—*dragons!* Sometimes called wyrms, these are dangerous winged reptiles who covet treasure and slay any who cross their paths. They are spoken of in whispers by common townsfolk, and legends are told of those who battled them and lived. A young dragon can terrify a village, while an ancient wyrm can lay waste to an entire army.

Evil dragons are chromatic—white, green, black, blue, and red. Each has different abilities and breath weapons, and uses a different environment as a lair. If you seek a reputation as a slayer of dragons, understanding these differences might save your life.

The size and power of a dragon depends on its age, which also determines its danger level. Wyrmlings are baby dragons, younger than 5 years, who are as tall as a human and quite vulnerable. Young dragons are 6 to 100 years old and between eight and sixteen feet tall. An adult dragon is 101 to 800 years old and between sixteen and thirty-two feet tall. Ancient dragons are older than 800 years. These gargantuan terrors are more than thirty-two feet tall, and some can reach forty feet or larger.

All adult dragons can beat their wings so powerfully that they create gusts of wind to knock over targets. They also have powerful jaws that can rend flesh and bone, as well as incredibly sharp claws that are able to pierce non-magical armor with ease. Larger dragons can swing their tails like massive prehensile clubs, battering foes to the ground. And older dragons generate a supernatural fear that can terrify their opponents just by being near them.

WHITE DRAGON

3-5

SPECIAL POWERS

COLD BREATH
These cold-hearted dragons can exhale a terrifying icy blast that can tear a target apart with chunks of ice or freeze them solid.

ICE WALK
White dragons can walk across ice and snow without slipping or getting stuck.

White dragons might be the smallest, least intelligent, and most primitive of the evil chromatic dragon types, but don't let that fool you into thinking they're easy to defeat. Driven by hunger and greed, they are viciously cruel reptiles who live in cold climates.

These pale dragons may not have the same level of tactics and cunning as their more intelligent cousins, but their animalistic nature makes them skilled hunters. Once they decide on a target, white dragons stay incredibly focused on their prey, letting nothing get in the way of the kill.

LAIR White dragons live in icy caves and deep subterranean chambers far from the light of the sun. They love vertical heights in their caverns and will sometimes fly up and latch on to the ceiling like huge bats. Older white dragons naturally give off magic that lowers the temperature around them, leeching heat from the surrounding area.

White dragons eat only frozen food. They use their devastating ice-breath attack to flash-freeze victims, then store their prey inside their icy lairs to serve as snacks when they're hungry.

DO THIS

Stay warm. White dragons will try to slow you down by chilling you to the bone or freezing you solid. Make sure to dress warmly when hunting these frosty foes.

Watch your step! With ice and snow everywhere in a white dragon's lair, it's easy to slip and lose your footing.

DON'T DO THIS

Don't tell them your name. White dragons are the most vengeful of all chromatic dragons. They never forget a face and can carry a grudge for as long as they live. If you tick off a white dragon, it'll come after you looking for revenge!

Don't underestimate them. They may be less intelligent than other chromatic dragons, but they're still incredibly dangerous!

GREEN DRAGON

3-5

SPECIAL POWERS

POISON BREATH
These stinky dragons can exhale a grotesque cloud of green gas that makes creatures ill and causes them to choke as they gasp for air.

AMPHIBIOUS
Green dragons can breathe underwater, and some of them hunt by springing up from hiding places beneath the surface of lakes or large ponds.

Green dragons are the most cunning and treacherous of all the evil chromatic dragons. They're nasty tempered and aggressive, eager to take territory and show off their power. They have long necks and legs, so they easily step over underbrush in forests and poke their heads up through the trees while keeping all four feet on the ground.

Intelligent and cruel, green dragons enjoy hunting and proving their superiority. If a target is weak, they'll happily torment their prey, holding off on the final kill until they've had their fun. Green dragons will eat any creature they kill, but their absolute favorite meal is elves, fresh and choking on poison from the dragon's toxic-breath attack.

LAIR Green dragons lurk in old forests and, over time, their presence will bring a disgusting-smelling fog to the area. They look for caves to turn into lairs, and some even dig out their own and then cover the entrance with thick vegetation.

DO THIS

Use your nose. Look out for smelly fog when traveling in a forest. It's a clear sign that a green dragon may be lurking nearby.

Watch out from all directions. Green dragons can attack from the air above the tree line or by quickly slipping through the forest to strike. They're built to use the trees to their advantage.

DON'T DO THIS

Don't get poisoned. As soon as you see a green dragon start to inhale, cover your face with a cloak or other material and try to get out of the way of its poison breath. The choking, stinging fog will obscure your sight and leave you open to attack!

Don't underestimate them! If a green dragon thinks it's going to lose a fight, it will quickly surrender and may even act helpful, but it's just looking for an opportunity to regain its advantage and destroy the heroes that brought it low.

GREEN DRAGON

Krydle pressed himself against the moss-covered tree and tried to stay still. If he moved, Goreedus the dragon would know he was there.

Goreedus craned his long, scaled neck around the twisted branches, looking through the marshy forest for any sign of disturbance. The dragon's piercing emerald eyes could see insects flitting in the stagnant air and tadpoles swimming perfect little circles in the water, but nothing else. No sign of the cloaked thief it detected mere moments ago.

"Human . . . I know you are hiding . . . hoping I will leave you to carry on your pitiful life."

Krydle disagreed with the "pitiful" descriptor, but the rest was accurate.

"In a few moments, I will breathe a cloud of poison that will make you choke and vomit, revealing your location. Then I will grab you with a clawed hand and rend you limb from limb."

That sounded quite unpleasant. Krydle's nose furrowed.

"If you step forth now and show yourself, I will ask you three questions and then grant you mercy. If you stay hidden, there is only death."

Krydle had seconds to decide: Reveal himself and hope for the best, or quietly take a deep breath and try not to ingest in any of the toxic fumes about to fill the air all around him?

What should Krydle do? If he steps forward, does the dragon instantly attack or does it give him a chance to negotiate? What could Krydle even say to keep a dragon from eating him? On the other hand, if Krydle holds his breath, what happens when the dragon's poison cloud lasts longer than he can manage without air? It's up to you!

BLACK DRAGON

3-5

SPECIAL POWERS

ACID BREATH
These dragons can exhale
a spray of burning acid,
scorching anyone unlucky
enough to be hit by it.

AMPHIBIOUS
Black dragons can breathe underwater,
and some hunt by lying in wait beneath
fetid and murky waters in large swamps.

Black dragons are the most sadistic of all the evil chromatic dragons. They enjoy destruction, and revel in turning vibrant places into rotting holes of decay.

Black dragons hate weakness and gleefully slay their most vulnerable enemies first, ensuring a quick and brutal victory. They cannot stand to be defeated or dominated, and would rather die than call someone else their "master."

LAIR You can find black dragons in rotting swamps or crumbling ruins, places that perfectly reflect their own destructive desires. Carrion eaters and insects tend to gather where black dragons live, cleaning the bones of the dragons' many rotting victims.

Over time, the land near a black dragon's lair will grow thick with twisted plants and reeking mud. Any sources of water near the dragon's lair will become corrupted and undrinkable, stained by the wyrm's foul presence.

DO THIS

Watch for ruins! Black dragons use ruins and swamps as their homes, so pay attention when exploring ancient places or marshlands.

Protect your group. Black dragons will focus on adventurers who aren't wearing armor, looking to exploit weakness. Make sure healers and magic-users are well protected, and keep armored combatants up front.

DON'T DO THIS

Don't get burned! Protect exposed flesh from nasty acid burns. Wear a heavy cloak and be prepared to cover yourself if the creature unleashes its powerful breath attack.

Don't underestimate them. Black dragons would rather die than surrender. In the final stages of a battle, a black dragon may lash out with desperation, so be careful!

BLUE DRAGON

3-5

SPECIAL POWERS

LIGHTNING BREATH
Blue dragons can exhale bolts of
lightning that scorch and blind foes.

SAND CLOUDS
Older blue dragons can summon
clouds of stinging sand to blind
and confuse their enemies.

Blue dragons are the most patient and methodical of all the evil chromatic dragons. They build their lairs patiently and hunt prey slowly and tactfully. A blue dragon knows that time is on its side, and its power will overtake almost any foe in the long run.

These dragons are the most likely to hire evil minions to help enact their schemes. They may covet gemstones and jewelry, but they know the value of a good servant too, and are willing to sacrifice from their treasure hoard to reward loyal service.

LAIR Blue dragons tend to live in desolate areas—badlands, broken steppes, and deserts. They build elaborate caves of crystal by using their lightning breath to fuse sand into shimmering caverns beneath the earth.

Thunder and lightning tend to gather near the lairs of older blue dragons, as do sand storms and tornados. The loud wind and booming air make for perfect cover when a blue dragon attacks unwary visitors.

DO THIS

Check the weather. Storm clouds or whipping winds in a desert may be signs that a blue dragon lives nearby.

Close the gap. Blue dragons have an advantage if they avoid close combat, so they keep their distance and pummel enemies with powerful bolts of lightning. Move in as soon as you can and don't let them escape!

DON'T DO THIS

Don't show your bling. Blue dragons collect gemstones—the larger and more valuable, the better. If they see you have pretty gemstones, they might just make you their next target.

Don't lose your temper. Blue dragons are patient and methodical in both schemes and battles. They expect their enemies to get emotional and make mistakes. Stay focused and try not to let the dragon control the flow of battle.

RED DRAGON

3-5

SPECIAL POWERS

VOLCANIC ACTIVITY
Older red dragons can make the ground shake with their roar or summon spouts of burning magma from beneath the earth. Losing in a battle against a red dragon means being burned alive or crushed beneath giant steaming rocks.

FIRE BREATH
Red dragons exhale gouts of deadly flame from deep within their bodies. The heat generated can easily melt flesh and burn clothes and even armor.

Red dragons are the most greedy and vain of all the evil chromatic dragons. They gather huge treasure hoards and possess huge egos to match. They remember every item they've plundered and can recall every foe who dared to stand against them.

Arrogant, possessive, and sometimes quite impulsive, red dragons prove their superiority by gathering information on enemies before striking with ruthless fury. They see themselves as the kings of dragonkind, with lesser dragons and all other creatures as mere slaves for them to command.

LAIR Red dragons frequently build lairs in mountains or hills, sometimes within deep mines or former dwarven strongholds. Volcanic caves are the most prized by red dragons, as these provide warm gasses that the reptiles find enjoyable and add protection against any intruders foolish enough to trespass.

Unnatural earthquakes may occur in the area around the lair of an older red dragon. Sources of water tend to be warmer than normal and may even be contaminated by sulfur.

DO THIS

Watch out for tremors! If you feel the earth shaking, you may be getting close to a red dragon's lair!

Flatter them. Red dragons have tremendous egos. If you get caught by a red dragon, heaping praise on them might give you extra time needed to devise an escape plan!

DON'T DO THIS

Don't get burned. Red dragons are creatures of fire. Confronting one means you'd better be prepared, with lots of armor and protective magic to keep from getting burned.

Don't steal! Red dragons are obsessed with their treasure hoards and will hunt thieves to the ends of the earth. If you take something that's theirs, you better know what you're doing!

TIAMAT, THE QUEEN OF EVIL DRAGONS

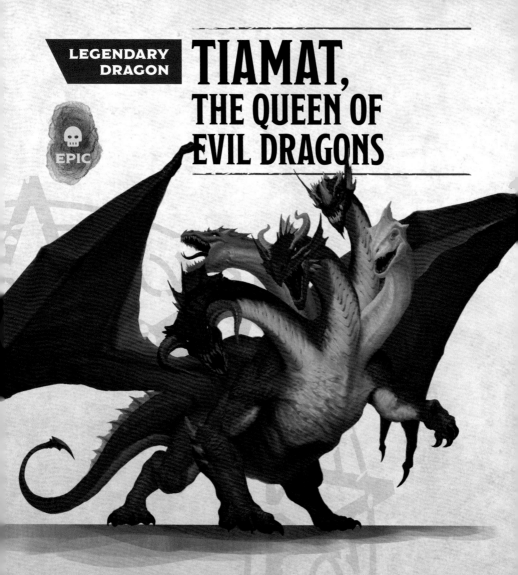

LAIR Tiamat lives in Avernus, a desolate dimension of war where devils battle each other in forsaken lands while fiery comets streak through the sky. In this foreboding realm stands Tiamat's temple, which has five separate spires—one for each evil dragon color.

Despite her incredible power, Tiamat is trapped in Avernus by an ancient curse. Her many followers strive to break the curse and set her free, so she may destroy all who oppose her. If they succeed, no one is safe!

Tiamat is the legendary and terrifying Queen of Evil Dragons. Her five heads, one for each of the evil dragon types, all share the same mind and have the same goal—to rule over all creatures and mortals, bringing about an apocalyptic Age of Dragons that would plunge the world into destructive chaos.

A regular dragon is one of the most terrifying opponents an adventurer can ever face, and Tiamat terrifies even other dragons. Just being in her presence can be enough to send most heroes running away screaming. Only the most courageous or foolhardy would ever fight the dragon queen and hope to succeed.

FIGHTING TIAMAT Tiamat is a massive multiheaded dragon with huge wings, powerful claws, and a vicious stinging tail. She cannot be hurt by non-magical weapons, and heals quickly from damage. Her five heads can each unleash a deadly breath weapon based on its dragon type.

Black: Burning acid sprays

Blue: Crackling lightning bolts

Green: Poisonous gas clouds

Red: Gouts of burning fire

White: Freezing ice blasts

Tiamat is one of the most dangerous creatures in all of existence. She is ancient, cunning, powerful, and merciless. Defeating the Queen of Evil Dragons would take an incredible amount of power or an army, or both.

SIZE Tiamat is approximately sixty feet long, which means she's one-third longer and taller than even the largest ancient chromatic dragon.

USING MONSTERS
TO TELL YOUR OWN STORIES

"Get ready, Boo!"

Boo the hamster squee'ed in a manner that made it abundantly clear he was not ready and probably never would be.

"Bones behind us and water below, it's time to jump!"

Minsc bombastically leapt off the top of the tower as the arrows of undead archers zipped past his face and skeletal hands grasped his tattered cloak.

As gravity quick took hold and they started to plummet toward the waves, the legendary ranger wondered if he'd make it back to Baldur's Gate in time for breakfast.

Reading about monsters kick-starts your imagination, doesn't it? With each entry, with every illustration, you start to create little stories in your mind. What happened before, what happens right after? These questions create an exciting daydream that can't stay contained.

All those wandering thoughts about action and adventure, they're the perfect way to begin building your own stories!

Your idea might start with a monster, but it can go *anywhere*: the creature's lair, the village nearby, cities and dungeons, caverns or skyscapes. You get to choose all the ingredients and stir them together. To help you as you develop your story, here are some questions to keep in mind:

WHO ARE YOUR CHARACTERS?

- Are your heroes like you or different? Young or old, human or something else? Think about the foes you must face. Great heroes require great challenges. What makes your villains memorable and powerful, and what brings them into conflict with your adventurers?

WHERE DOES YOUR STORY TAKE PLACE?

- At the top of a mountain, in a serene forest, deep underwater, or in a creepy boneyard?

WHEN DOES THE STORY HAPPEN?

- At night or during the day, in the middle of a thunderstorm or right before the bells toll to ring in the new year? Think about time passing as your story unfolds.

HOW DO THINGS CHANGE AS THE STORY PROCEEDS?

- Do your heroes succeed or fail? Do they find somewhere new or explore someplace old?

WHAT SHOULD SOMEONE FEEL AS THEY EXPERIENCE YOUR STORY?

- Do you want them to laugh or get scared? Cheer or be grossed out?

WHY ARE YOUR HEROES GOING ON THIS ADVENTURE?

- Knowing what their goals are will help you create a compelling tale of heroism and exploration.

Remember, you don't have to answer all these questions by yourself! DUNGEONS & DRAGONS is a collaborative game where you work with your friends to create your own stories. One person acts as a narrator, called a Dungeon Master, and the other players each take on the role of a hero, called a Player Character, in the adventuring party in a story. The Dungeon Master sets up a scene by describing a place and any threats that may exist, and then each player contributes ideas by explaining their own character's actions. With each scene created by the group, the story moves forward in unexpected and entertaining ways.

If you don't feel confident starting from scratch, you can go to your local gaming store and play a DUNGEONS & DRAGONS demonstration session. Demos can be a quick way to learn how the game is played and an opportunity to possibly make some brand-new friends at the same time.

After you've read through all the creatures in this little monster manual, there's even more DUNGEONS & DRAGONS material to ignite your imagination, the *Warriors & Weapons* guide is packed with character ideas and equipment to outfit your courageous adventurer. You know what dangers lurk in the darkness, now figure out who your hero will be and *fight them back*!

Published in the United States by Ten Speed Press, an imprint of Random House, a division of Penguin Random House LLC, New York.
www.crownpublishing.com
www.tenspeed.com

Ten Speed Press and the Ten Speed Press colophon are registered trademarks of Penguin Random House LLC.

Originally published in the United States in hardcover by Ten Speed Press, an imprint of Random House, a division of Penguin Random House LLC, New York, in 2019.

Publisher: Aaron Wehner
Art Director and Designer: Betsy Stromberg
Editors: Patrick Barb and Julie Bennett
Managing Editor: Doug Ogan
Production Designer: Lisa Bieser
Wizards of the Coast Team: David Gershman, Kate Irwin, Adam Lee, Hilary Ross, Liz Schuh
Illustrations: Conceptopolis, LLC

10 9 8 7

2020 Trade Paperback Boxed Set Edition

WIZARDS & SPELLS

DUNGEONS & DRAGONS

WIZARDS &
SPELLS

A Young Adventurer's Guide

WRITTEN BY JIM ZUB
WITH STACY KING AND ANDREW WHEELER

TEN SPEED PRESS
California | New York

CONTENTS

INTRODUCTION

You are in a fantasy realm. That means there are fantastical creatures and even more fantastical abilities.

What kind of magic do you wield?

How will you use your powers?

This book is a way to answer those two very important questions. It's a guide to the extraordinary abilities that enhance the world of DUNGEONS & DRAGONS and the magic-centered classes available to adventurers. It gives you a wide range of options to choose from, along with spells and magical items to outfit your heroic persona.

Read this book from start to finish, or open it to any spot, get pulled in by the exciting illustrations, and start brainstorming from there. The more you read, the more character ideas will spring from your imagination.

Every character is unique. Even when two of them share the same magical vocation, the decisions they make will take them on an exclusive journey that is yours to tell. DUNGEONS & DRAGONS is all about building memorable characters, and the tales of your magical exploits are about to begin.

Let's explore!

BARD

CLERIC

DRUID

SORCERER

WARLOCK

WIZARD

CHARACTER CLASSES

Character class is a major defining element for a well-developed persona. You can think of it as your job, although it involves more than just work. A character's class shapes their education, skills, and abilities. It will also guide how characters interact with each other. Each class has stereotypes (good and bad) that affect whether your character is seen as trustworthy or deceptive, loyal or unreliable. In the case of magic users, who are the focus of this book, class can also affect the nature of their magic and the kinds of spells they are able to cast.

In addition, your character will belong to one of twelve races, ranging from humans, elves, or dwarves to tabaxi (cat folk), kenku (bird people), or half-orcs (see *Warriors & Weapons* for more details). Although some races are better suited to certain classes than others, your character can be any combination you want. It can be fun to spend some time dreaming up a creative history to explain how your character gained the training and skills needed for their chosen class!

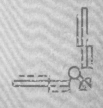

BARD

DO YOU BELIEVE THERE
IS MAGIC IN MUSIC?

DO YOU OFTEN FIND
YOURSELF THE CENTER
OF ATTENTION?

DO YOU LOVE
TO PERFORM?

YOU MIGHT BE A BARD!

BARDIC COLLEGES

Bards may learn music and magic on the road, from a mentor, or with formal schooling. All bards belong to informal associations called *Colleges*, through which they share their stories and traditions. There are two Colleges.

COLLEGE OF LORE
These bards believe in the power of words to change the world. They are smart, sharp, witty, and adept at casting spells.

COLLEGE OF VALOR
These bards believe in the power of deeds to change the world. They seek to inspire others through their actions, and to keep the stories of great heroes alive.

Traveling from town to town, singing songs and telling tales, bardic life is traditionally associated with the adventures of other people spun into stories that a bard will tell or sing in exchange for a few coins. Yet there are many bards who pursue a life of adventure themselves. After all, what could be more glorious than singing songs where *you* are the star?

Bards understand that story and song have the power to reshape reality. There is magic in these gifts, and bards harness that magic to achieve great deeds. A talent for music is something all bards share, but playing an instrument and singing songs are not the only styles of performance available to them. You might prefer to be a poet, an actor, an acrobat, a dancer, or a clown.

Although most bards prefer to assist their allies from the sidelines, they are able to defend themselves with spells that enhance both weapons and armor. That said, their magic leans toward charms and illusions rather than destructive power. The end of a life is the end of a story, after all, and bards tend to believe that there is always a chance for redemption so long as a story continues to be told.

EQUIPMENT AND ATTRIBUTES

Armor Bards tend to travel light, using only leather or studded-leather armor.

Weapons They favor graceful defenses such as rapiers, swords, and hand crossbows, along with daggers, hand axes, and slings.

Musical Instruments Almost all bards play some sort of musical instrument, from a simple reed flute to an elegant harp, and their instruments can be used in spellcasting.

Music as Magic A bard's magical music can have many effects, including healing the sick, charming others, or freeing people from mind control.

Inspirational Gifts Bards use music and song to inspire others around them to perform great deeds. If a member of your party is struggling, a bard will often know exactly what they need to hear to turn their fortunes around!

FLORIZAN BLANK

PLAYING FLORIZAN BLANK Florizan hates bullies and tyrants, and loves beauty and art. He's warm, charming, and quick to adapt to new situations. He enjoys talking to people to get a sense of their stories and experiences. Having seen life from both the palace and the gutter, Florizan knows that truth and kindness are free to every person, no matter their possessions or wealth.

As the youngest son of a royal family in a small southern kingdom, Florizan Blank studied music, poetry, and dance from an early age. When he was 10 years old, his family was overthrown by traitors; Florizan was the only survivor. Smuggled out of the palace by his music teacher, he was given a new identity and raised in a traveling circus, where he learned bardic magic. He gained a reputation as a great actor, and it was in this role that fortune brought him back to the palace where he had lived as a child.

Florizan saw an opportunity. He wrote and performed a play that exposed the tyrant's crimes and incited a revolution. When offered the chance to retake his throne, Florizan refused, preferring life on the road.

DANDY DUELIST Florizan's stylish appearance and way with words have led many opponents to underestimate him as a fighter, yet his dance training has made him an excellent swordsman. His favorite move is to cast a dancing enchantment on his foe, so that a fight to the death becomes a flamboyant two-step—to the amazement and amusement of anyone watching—until Florizan delivers the finishing blow!

BLANK MASK

Florizan carries a simple pink carnival mask that was given to him by a grateful witch after he used his powers of persuasion to save her from execution. When Florizan wears the mask, he can magically alter his appearance for up to an hour. He uses this mask to impersonate other people or to create fictional individuals from his own imagination.

CLERIC

DO YOU HAVE A CLEAR
PURPOSE IN LIFE?

DO YOU SEEK TO INSPIRE
THOSE AROUND YOU?

DO YOU DESIRE TO SERVE
A HIGHER POWER?

YOU MIGHT BE A CLERIC!

DIVINE DOMAINS
Each cleric is devoted to one specific god and each god is devoted to one particular idea or principle. The magic on which clerics draw is tied to these divine domains. Most divine magic falls into one of six domains.

LIFE
Gods that care most for the preservation of life. These clerics are expert healers.

LIGHT
Gods of beauty, rebirth, and the sun. These clerics use cleansing fire and blinding light.

NATURE
Gods of the harvest and the forest. These clerics access nature magic, and can control animals and plants.

TEMPEST
Gods of storms and weather. These clerics can summon lightning or command powerful winds.

TRICKERY
Gods of mischief and subversion. These clerics may alter their appearance or slip between shadows.

WAR
Gods of chivalry and battle. These clerics use magic to strike their enemies hard and fast!

Gods are a very real presence in the worlds of DUNGEONS & DRAGONS, and they can bestow blessings and power upon their most faithful followers. Among these faithful are the clerics who act as earthly servants of their chosen deity, and who are able to channel divine magic to heal the injured, protect the weak, and smite the wicked.

A cleric's magic is defined by the nature of the god they serve. They wear their gods' symbols, fight in their gods' name, and live every day according to the principles of their faith. This doesn't necessarily mean that they're reserved or quiet characters. Some gods are very raucous and wild!

Clerics will often follow their god's call to set off on an adventure, perhaps to right a wrong, vanquish a foe, or bring home a lost relic. Wherever they go, clerics take their god and their faith with them.

EQUIPMENT AND ATTRIBUTES

Armor Clerics are the chosen warriors of their gods, and often don heavy armor.

Weapons They carry formidable instruments of war, such as swords, hammers, or crossbows.

Holy Symbols Each god has a symbol that is sacred to its faith, and clerics will not only wear these symbols on their armor but also carry physical representations of them, such as a talisman or an engraved shield.

Channeling Divinity Clerics draw on the powers of their gods to cast their magic. The effects vary according to the type of god they serve, and can include powers of healing, destruction, deception, and light.

Destroying the Undead Clerics are the scourge of undead creatures, whose existence is an insult to all the gods. Clerics can channel their divine powers through their holy symbols to drive the undead away or to destroy them.

BEL VALA

PLAYING BEL VALA Bel Vala is a devout follower of Corellon, the patron god of elves and the protector of life, and she takes her faith very seriously. She believes that Corellon is the source of her strength and her survival. She also considers life to be a holy gift that one must never be quick to take away, even in combat.

HEALING OVER HARM Bel Vala is not enthusiastic about martial combat. She prefers to play the role of healer, focusing her time and energy to ensure her friends and allies prosper. The exception is when she faces the undead. In those instances, Bel Vala is a remorseless warrior who channels a divine light that can eradicate their evil.

Bel Vala was a young novice healer in Tower Crystalis when the earthquake came. Inexperienced and unsure of her strength, Bel found herself trapped among the sick and dying after the tower collapsed. Next came the flood waters, bringing with them an ancient evil. Suddenly, the dead were walking again. The broken tower was filled with abominations seeking to feed on the few remaining survivors.

Bel Vala prayed to her god, Corellon, for guidance. Inspired, she channeled a cleansing light through her body into the fallen shards of the crystal tower, where it refracted a thousand times. The undead were destroyed by this incredible burst of divine power.

Bel Vala woke years later from a deep sleep. She had lost her sight but gained a new clarity of purpose. She was Corellon's humble champion, protector of the living and bane to all undead.

DIVINE VISION Though completely blind, Bel Vala has refined her divination skills to an extraordinary degree, allowing her to sense the thoughts and intentions of those around her. Bel Vala believes that Corellon will guide her through danger and lead her to where she needs to be.

THE CHALICE, THE BOOK, AND THE DAGGER

Bel Vala has been named the caretaker of a set of linked items, said to have belonged to Corellon, which she can summon from a fold of light.

The chalice is Taker, and anyone who drinks from it can be relieved of all mundane injuries and illnesses. The book is Keeper, which keeps a record of those afflictions. The dagger is Giver, and it can pass those afflictions on to anyone it touches. Bel Vala must balance the book by each new moon, or any afflictions recorded in the book will pass on to her.

DRUID

DO YOU FEEL A STRONG
CONNECTION TO NATURE?

DO YOU CARE PASSIONATELY
ABOUT THE ENVIRONMENT?

DO YOU LOVE ANIMALS SO
MUCH THAT YOU WISH YOU
COULD BE ONE?

YOU MIGHT BE A DRUID!

DRUID CIRCLES
Many druids belong to one of two major traditions that define their practices and grant them special abilities.

CIRCLE OF LAND
Druids in this order are attuned to the power of the earth beneath their feet. They use this power to fuel magic and access spells unique to their home turf. For example, a druid from the grasslands may be an expert at passing undetected, while a druid living near the sea may have a talent for breathing underwater.

CIRCLE OF THE MOON
Druids in this order draw on the power of the moon to enhance their ability to transform into animals. They are especially skilled at using their wild-shape powers in combat, and they can transform into exceptionally ferocious beasts, ones beyond the abilities of other druids.

Druids are champions of the natural world. By attuning themselves to the elements, or by serving the gods who protect nature, they can unlock great mystical powers, including the ability to transform into beasts.

Druids care most about living in peace with nature and maintaining a balance between earth, air, fire, and water. They often defend wildernesses and sacred sites from unwanted intruders, fighting those who would try to control, abuse, or corrupt the natural world—especially undead abominations and unnatural monsters.

Druids are most likely to pursue a life of adventure when they feel the balance of nature is disturbed or that the harmony of their existence is under threat. They feel a sacred duty to the life force that runs through all things, and they will pursue that duty to the best of their ability.

EQUIPMENT AND ATTRIBUTES

Armor Druids use armor and shields made from natural materials such as wood and leather.

Weapons They prefer light, simple arms that have everyday uses in the wilderness, such as spears and slings for hunting or knives and sickles for harvesting. They also favor wooden weapons, or weapons with wooden handles.

Nature Magic Druidic spells harness the power of the natural world, such as exerting control over the weather and the elements, summoning and speaking to animals, and controlling the surrounding environment.

Wild Shape Druids can transform into animals and take on that animal's abilities. This can include land animals such as tigers and bulls, swimming creatures such as dolphins and sharks, and flying creatures such as eagles and bats, or even a swarm of bees! Most druids can't use their other skills, such as spellcasting, while in animal form.

DAWAN PAX

PLAYING DAWAN PAX Dawan Pax is both a devoted ally of nature and a powerful half-orc fighter. These aspects of his character manifest in the fierce and sometimes brutal way he defends and avenges his animal friends He prefers the company of animals; and he does not eat meat, which is unusual for a half-orc.

WIND THROUGH THE GRASS Despite his considerable size, Dawan Pax can move silently and stealthily through wild terrain, at times even becoming magically invisible. He retains the grace and athleticism of the beasts into which he transforms.

M any strange stories have been told about Dawan Pax, a half-orc also known as The Hunter's Curse for his sabotage of sporting hunts. Some say he was raised by beasts, and that's why he protects them. Others say he's a simple-minded brute who knows no other life. Still others believe that he doesn't exist at all, and he's merely a superstition created to scare strangers away from the wilds. None of these stories are true, and many of them were designed to belittle the fearsome druid—because few hunters have ever found any other way to defeat him.

The truth is, Pax lived an unremarkable life in a small orcish village, where he was raised to be a hunter. His closest friend was an old gray wolf who lived near the village in peace and harmony with the people.

One day, outsiders slaughtered the wolf. Pax found the body. In that moment, he devoted himself to search out the hunters and end their sport. In the pursuit of this end, he has traveled to many lands, becoming a great warrior and honing his druidic arts.

HONORING THE BEASTS Dawan Pax often uses his wild shape to live among the animals he protects. He has also been known to pursue hunters in the forms of animals they have killed. To this day, he still sometimes takes the shape of the old gray wolf.

THE SOUL OF THE EARTH

Dawan Pax carries an ancient piece of polished volcanic stone called the Soul of the Earth, which allows him to cast a particularly advanced form of *scrying* spell. If Pax recovers an arrow or other projectile from an injured creature, he can use the Soul of the Earth to summon a vision of the person who attacked the animal. He retains this vision even when in animal form, allowing him to track down his new enemy.

SORCERER

DO STRANGE THINGS HAPPEN WHEN YOU'RE AROUND?

DO YOU COPE POSITIVELY WITH UNCERTAINTY AND CHAOS?

DO YOU TRUST YOUR INTUITION?

YOU MIGHT BE A **SORCERER!**

DRACONIC BLOODLINES

Draconic-bloodline magic comes from the intersection of a dragon's magic with either you or your ancestors. As you learn to channel this magic, the imprint of the dragon will begin to manifest. At first, you will be able to speak draconic, the ancient language of dragons. As your power grows, dragonlike scales will appear on your skin, increasing your resistance to damage. Powerful draconic-bloodline sorcerers have even been known to sprout dragon wings that allow them to fly!

Your draconic ancestor can be one of any of the different types of dragons, and your magic will be influenced by the dragon you select. See *Monsters & Creatures* for more details about dragon types and their powers.

Sorcerers are born with an innate magic, one they did not choose but cannot deny. This magic may come from a draconic bloodline, an otherworldly influence, or exposure to unknown cosmic forces. In some cases, the sorcerer may have no idea why or how their magic developed, leading them on a lifelong quest to uncover the source of their power. This wild magic (see page 74) can be unpredictable and dangerous, with startling side effects at the most awkward moments.

Most sorcerers find themselves drawn to a life of adventure sooner rather than later. The magic in their veins does not like to lie dormant. Those who don't learn to channel their power may find their gifts spilling out anyway, in unexpected and often unpleasant ways.

EQUIPMENT AND ATTRIBUTES

Armor Too much gear can interfere with a sorcerer's magic, so they wear no armor.

Weapons They can use only simple armaments such as daggers, darts, quarterstaffs, and light crossbows.

Font of Magic The deep wellspring of magic within each sorcerer allows them to cast magical spells at will. Fledgling sorcerers begin with the power to cast a few spells each day. As they gain more understanding of their inner magic, that number increases.

Metamagic Unlike spells learned by rote memorization, a sorcerer's magic is intuitive and flexible. With a little experience under their belts, they can learn to alter spells to suit their needs. Some examples of metamagic include shielding allies from a spell's effects, extending the range of damage done, or allowing the spell to be cast silently rather than spoken aloud.

DAMINI MAHAJAN

PLAYING DAMINI MAHAJAN

Like her draconic ancestor, Damini can be proud. She does not tolerate disrespect, especially from those who need her help. When approached politely, she is warm and welcoming, surprisingly down-to-earth for a sorcerer who literally spends all day with her head in the clouds. The air around her cackles faintly with energy and a pale blue light, reflecting the magic held within her diminutive frame.

LIGHTNING ELEMENTALS

Damini can summon lightning elementals to fight on her behalf or to assist with her occult research. These creatures, formed from actual lightning into a humanoid shape, remain for up to one hour after summoning and only obey Damini's commands. These dangerous elementals are attracted to metal and will damage any living flesh that they touch.

Born to a long line of draconic sorcerers descended from a powerful blue dragon, Damini Mahajan displays an extraordinary control over lightning. Her powers manifested at an early age, and she spent her childhood learning to transform tiny sparks into crackling bolts of electricity. Now in her seventies, her mastery over this volatile element has reached the level of legend.

Damini is best known for her leadership in the war against the Batiri, a tribe of goblin fighters lead by Queen M'bobo to invade the neighboring kingdom. In a desperate last stand, when the rest of her party had been knocked unconscious, Damini summoned a lightning storm so powerful that it killed more than eighty goblins with a single blast. The backlash from her spell left the distinctive spiral scar that still marks one side of her face.

Although her three children did not inherit her magic, the power has manifested in two of her grandchildren. Damini has dedicated her remaining days to training them as the next generation of Mahajan sorcerers.

MAHAJAN TOWER

Damini lives in Mahajan Tower near the peak of Mount Pentos, where she can be close to the clouds that fuel her research. Two of her grandchildren reside with her in the spiraling column, learning to control their own magical abilities. From time to time, Damini takes on students from outside her family line, teaching them to understand and master their newfound mystical talents.

WARLOCK

ARE YOU DRIVEN TO PURSUE KNOWLEDGE, WHATEVER THE COST?

ARE YOU ABLE TO BACK UP YOUR MAGIC WITH PHYSICAL FIGHTING SKILLS?

ARE YOU PREPARED TO SERVE SOMEONE ELSE'S WILL IN TRADE FOR POWER?

YOU MIGHT BE A WARLOCK!

PACT BOON Once warlocks have proven their loyalty, their patrons grant them a special ability known as a pact boon. This gift may take one of three forms.

PACT OF THE BLADE
The warlock learns to create a magical melee weapon out of thin air, so they are never unarmed.

PACT OF THE CHAIN
The warlock is taught a spell that allows them to summon a magical familiar, a spirit that looks like a small animal and obeys the warlock's commands.

PACT OF THE TOME
The warlock is gifted with a magical book, called a grimoire, that contains three spells the warlock can always cast, so long as the book is in their possession.

W arlocks are driven by the pursuit of knowledge above all other things. Their power comes not from innate talent or long study, but by making a lifelong pact of service to an otherworldly force. These patrons, as they are called, can take a variety of shapes, from ancient magical creatures to dark beings from forgotten places.

Whether good, evil, or simply indifferent to mortal affairs, all patrons require a price from those they aid. This may be as simple as a few tasks here and there, or as complex as running a vast following devoted to the patron. In trade for their service, the warlock is given access to arcane wisdom and magics beyond the realm of most mortals.

Some warlocks enjoy a good relationship with their patron, like that between a teacher and a favored student. Others struggle with the demands placed on them by their pact. In either case, their powerful spells and deep occult insight make warlocks a valuable addition to any party, even if their true loyalty may sometimes be uncertain.

EQUIPMENT AND ATTRIBUTES

Armor Warlocks don't shy away from getting their hands dirty, and can wear light leather armor to get the job done.

Weapons They wield a range of simple weapons, such as daggers, shortbows, crossbows, and hand axes.

Eldritch Invocations Fragments of occult lore uncovered during a warlock's studies, these powerful incantations allow the warlock to cast certain spells with ease.

Pact Magic A warlock starts their adventures knowing two cantrips (see page 34) and two regular spells, taught to them by their patron, and learn more as they gain experience.

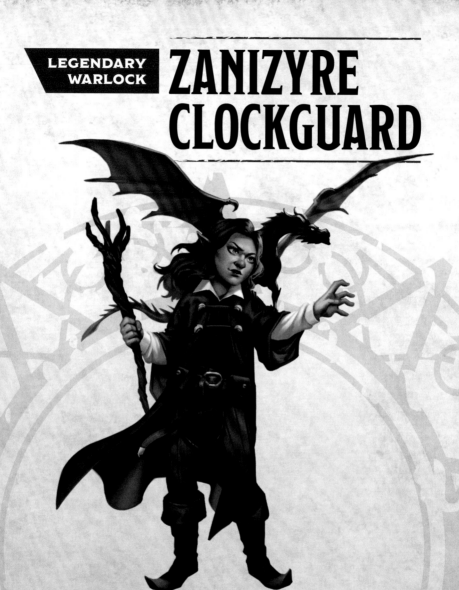

LEGENDARY WARLOCK

ZANIZYRE CLOCKGUARD

PLAYING ZANIZYRE CLOCKGUARD Zanizyre is naturally curious and cheerful, but the weight of her patron's evil often weighs on her, inspiring fits of melancholy. She does her best to help others and always takes the opportunity to do a good deed. However, she is unable to refuse her patron's requests. Since Tiamat is a creature bent on destruction, this means Zanizyre sometimes finds herself committing terrible crimes. Even so, she will refuse any attempts to be freed from Tiamat's service.

Fearsome warlock Zanizyre Clockguard is among the few mortals gifted with the patronage of Tiamat, the legendary Queen of Evil Dragons. There are many rumors as to how Zanizyre gained Tiamat's attention, but the most persistent tale is that she rescued an injured dragon hatchling and brought it to one of Tiamat's temples. Zanizyre refuses to answer questions on the matter, saying only that it was fate.

Driven to explore the world in her endless quest for knowledge, Zanizyre rarely stays in one place for long. She is known for using her magical powers to help the oppressed and downtrodden, and many a small town is grateful for her well-timed help against an invading force. Some say she is making amends for the terrible service demanded by her patron, for Tiamat is an evil creature dedicated to wiping out all mortal life.

DOMINATE DRAGON This powerful spell is a variation on the *dominate monster* spell (see page 66) and allows Zanizyre to force a dragon to do her bidding. Dragons are notoriously difficult to subdue with magic, between their resistant hides and own innate magical natures. Although Zanizyre rarely uses this spell, it always makes an impression. The sight of a three-foot-tall gnome charging into battle on the back of a mighty dragon is not easily forgotten!

TIAMAT'S FANG

Zanizyre's pact boon is a magical short sword known as Tiamat's Fang. This weapon can deliver damage related to each of Tiamat's five heads, allowing Zanizyre to choose between acid, lightning, poison, fire, or freezing effects each time she summons the weapon. This ability to tailor attacks to her opponent's weakness makes Zanizyre a deadly and unpredictable foe.

WIZARD

DO YOU ENJOY READING AND
STUDYING NEW THINGS?

DO YOU YEARN FOR A LIFE OF
MAGIC AND ADVENTURE?

DO YOU DESIRE
MAGICAL POWER?

YOU MIGHT BE A WIZARD!

A WIZARD'S SPELLBOOK A good spellbook is crucial to any wizard. You can write new spells in your book, expanding your powers with each new entry. Spellbooks can range in appearance from plain, travel-worn volumes to ornate tomes decorated with precious gemstones. No matter how fancy, the true value of a spellbook lies in the magic words written upon its pages!

If your spellbook is ever destroyed, you can recover only the spells you have currently memorized. For this reason, many wizards create a backup copy of their book, stored in a safe place while they are off adventuring.

Wizards are the supreme magic users, steeped in occult knowledge and trained extensively in the art of spellcasting. Fire and lightning are within their grasp, along with deceptive illusions and powerful mind control. The mightiest can command powers beyond imagination, including visions of the future and gateways that connect to strange dimensions beyond our reality.

For wizards, improving their spellcraft is their driving motivation; all else is secondary. They learn from many sources, including experimentation, libraries, mentors, and even ancient creatures willing to trade insight for personal favors. Most wizards spend years in intense study before embarking on their adventures.

However, unlike warlocks, wizards refuse to be bound in service to any creature or ideal. Their greatest personal treasure is their spellbook, where they make note of all the rituals, magical words, and arcane knowledge that they uncover during their travels.

EQUIPMENT AND ATTRIBUTES

Armor To effectively cast spells, a wizard must be able to move freely. Most wear no armor.

Weapons They use only simple defenses such as darts, slings, daggers, quarterstaffs, and light crossbows.

Spellbook Wizards begin with just six spells written in their spellbook, and can memorize two for quick use during a battle. They can switch up which spells they have memorized, but only when they have a few hours to rest and prepare.

Spellcasting Wizards have limits in their spellcasting power, although this grows as they gain experience. To begin with, a wizard can cast only a few spells before needing rest.

MORDENKAINEN

PLAYING MORDENKAINEN Brilliant and well-read, Mordenkainen does not tolerate fools. He prefers to listen rather than talk and is skilled at encouraging others to share their thoughts with him. When he does speak, his words evoke authority and confidence. He can be stubborn and difficult, and rarely changes his mind once he decides on a course of action.

A one-man peacekeeping force, Mordenkainen has created some of the most powerful spells known throughout the realms. His strong opposition to moral absolutes means that he can appear as a friend or foe, depending on his current goals and fickle mood. Above all, he is driven by a desire for balance, never letting the cosmic scales tip too far toward either good or evil.

Mordenkainen's origins are unknown, although he is thought to have been born along the Wild Coast of Greyhawk, an untamed land filled with hardship and danger. He came to prominence as the founder of the Citadel of Eight, a collective of magic users who sought to keep peace throughout the lands of Oerth. The Citadel disbanded after a hard-fought battle at the Temple of Elemental Evil, where one member lost his life. Two years later, Mordenkainen founded the Circle of Eight, which continues to operate under his guidance.

A skilled leader and political manipulator, Mordenkainen is always looking to expand his arcane understanding of good and evil as an agent of true neutrality.

MORDENKAINEN'S SPELLS

As one of the most powerful wizards to have ever lived, Mordenkainen is responsible for creating many new spells, including the following.

MORDENKAINEN'S MAGNIFICENT MANSION

This incantation creates an extradimensional dwelling that exists for up to twenty-four hours. The house appears with enough food to feed one hundred people and contains a staff of one hundred ghostly servants, although these specters cannot attack or leave the mansion.

MORDENKAINEN'S FAITHFUL HOUND

This spell summons a phantom watchdog that can see through illusions yet remains invisible to every creature but the spellcaster. The hound will remain for up to eight hours, although it will vanish if the spellcaster moves more than one hundred feet from the spot where the summoning occurred.

MORDENKAINEN'S SWORD

Casting this invocation conjures a shimmering elemental sword made of pure force, which hovers in the air before the spellcaster. The sword will deliver melee attacks against chosen targets on command. It lasts for one minute before dissolving.

CLASS FLOWCHART

IS YOUR MAGICAL POWER INNATE WITHIN YOU
OR DOES IT COME FROM TRAINING?

INNATE

Do you search for arcane secrets or
are you interested in nature?

SECRETS

NATURE

Is your magic personal or do you use it
for the benefit of a group?

PERSONAL

GROUP

YOU MIGHT BE A GOOD
SORCERER

YOU MIGHT BE A GOOD
BARD

YOU MIGHT BE A GOOD
DRUID

Choosing a character class can be difficult, so here's a little chart you can use to help you decide.

TRAINING

Will you readily serve the demands of another?

NO

YES

Is your cause one of faith or do you follow some other power?

FAITH

OTHER POWER

YOU MIGHT BE A GOOD
WIZARD

YOU MIGHT BE A GOOD
CLERIC

YOU MIGHT BE A GOOD
WARLOCK

TYPES OF MAGIC

Academies of magic and eldritch researchers have grouped spells and their effects into eight categories called the *schools of magic*. A magic user can learn spells from multiple schools, although they may find that certain types suit their aptitude and personality better than others.

Abjuration: Block attacks or negate harmful effects.

Conjuration: Transport objects and creatures or bring them into existence from thin air.

Divination: Reveal information such as forgotten secrets, the location of hidden things, or glimpses of future events.

Enchantment: Influence or control others through entrancement or commands.

Evocation: Manipulate magical energy to create a desired effect, including the creation of fire, lightning, or beams of light.

Illusion: Deceive the senses with magical trickery, right in front of one's eyes or sometimes inside the mind.

Necromancy: Use the cosmic forces of life, death, and undeath to strengthen or drain energy from a target.

Transmutation: Alter the nature of things or creatures from their original form.

There's another important way magic can be categorized: Arcane or Divine.

Arcane magic, used by wizards, warlocks, sorcerers, and bards, draws directly upon magical energies to produce their effects. Divine magic, used by clerics, druids, paladins, and rangers, is mediated by divine powers—gods, the primal forces of nature, or a paladin's sacred oath. Both types of magic can be quite potent.

RITUALS AND SCROLLS

Most spells are cast in the moment and unleash an immediate magical effect, but there are other ways to cast or store magic—via rituals and scrolls.

A *ritual* is a longer and more involved magical-casting process. It can be used to create increased and sometimes even permanent effects, such as warding a room against intruders. Some rituals involve rare components, carefully chosen locations, or even specific times of the day or alignments of stars and planets in the sky above.

A *scroll* is a spell stored in written form, waiting to be unleashed. Once used, the scroll is destroyed and cannot be used again.

Any creature who can understand a written language can activate a scroll. An adventuring party without a spellcaster can use scrolls to help with healing, protection, or other enchantments needed for their quest.

SPELLCASTING

Of the many different types of magic found in the worlds of DUNGEONS & DRAGONS, the most common are *spells*. A spell is a distinct magical effect created by a caster that alters the normal world in some fashion. Spells can be quite subtle or literally world-shaking in their purpose and power. A well-timed spell can turn the tide of a losing battle or save an adventuring party from ruin. As your hero travels, their magical abilities will grow as they learn new spells by training with a mentor, discovering ancient writings, or exploring their inner power.

Beginning spellcasters can use only cantrips and first-level spells, and they gain access to more powerful levels of magic as they test their abilities and grow in experience. Some spells can be used with any type of magic, while others require a connection to either Arcane or Divine power to be cast. Magic is complex, and so are the rules of which classes can cast specific spells.

Though magic-wielding heroes can access only a handful of spells at any one time, hundreds are available to them; and many more are waiting to be discovered or even created. There's no way to cover every spell imaginable, so our focus is on four spells for each level that will most benefit spellcasters as their powers develop.

CONCENTRATION

In the following profiles, there are spells where "concentration" is indicated. These spell effects can last longer than the instant they're cast, but only while a spellcaster maintains absolute focus on the magic being used.

CANTRIPS

Cantrips take very little power and concentration, allowing them to be used at will, unlike higher-level spells, which require the caster to rest after using their allotment. In this way, a spellcaster always has a bit of magic to help themselves or their allies in a tough situation.

MESSAGE SCHOOL: TRANSMUTATION

When you cast a *message* spell, you can point your finger at a creature or person within one hundred twenty feet of you, and they'll hear a message from you and be able to respond briefly. No one else can hear the messages, so it's the perfect way to communicate a quick idea in secret.

SPELL TIPS

- You can cast this spell if you know the location of your recipient, even if they're on the other side of a barrier.

- This spell can be blocked by thick stone, metal, or wood if they don't contain any gaps. But a *message* spell can travel around corners or through tiny openings.

- The creature you target with this spell needs to understand your language in order to communicate with you. This spell doesn't translate words, it only sends a message in a language you already know.

LIGHT
SCHOOL: EVOCATION

This basic spell makes an object glow with bright light for up to one hour. The target can be up to ten feet wide, creating a stationary light source. Alternatively, it can be something handheld that you carry with you. A *light* spell is a classic bit of spellcasting for good reason—it's always helpful to see where you're going in the dark!

SPELL TIPS

☞ The light can be any color you choose, so don't be afraid to get imaginative.

☞ Although the light this spell gives off is bright, it can be covered by a cloak or other obscuring material if necessary.

PRESTIDIGITATION

SCHOOL: TRANSMUTATION

Novice spellcasters use this minor magical trick to practice their spellcasting abilities. With *prestidigitation*, you can create one of these situations.

- An instant, harmless, and obviously magical effect such as a shower of sparks, puff of wind, faint musical notes, or a strange smell.

- Light or snuff out a candle, torch, or small campfire.

- Make a small object clean or dirty.

- Chill, warm up, or add flavor to food (about one cubic foot's worth).

- Mark with a symbol or add color to an object for up to an hour.

- Create a trinket or a small magical illusion in your hand for a few seconds.

SPELL TIPS

► If you cast this spell three times, you can have up to three different *prestidigitation* effects going simultaneously.

► This spell is an easy way to show off to commoners and build your reputation as powerful and mysterious. An imaginative use of *prestidigitation* can amuse or frighten people or creatures who don't know the ways of magic.

SHOCKING GRASP
SCHOOL: EVOCATION

The *shocking grasp* spell conjures a bit of electricity to deliver a jolt to the next creature or person you touch. It may look like a practical joke but, if you're lucky, this shock can knock down small creatures in one hit. Use it wisely and its zap will be one your foes remember!

SPELL TIPS

- This spell only works if you can touch your target (unlike *call lightning* on page 47, which is a more powerful spell that can hit targets farther away).

- If your opponent is wearing metal armor, this shock can be even more powerful, so pick your target wisely to maximize its effect.

FIRST LEVEL

These spells for novice magic wielders will give your character a bigger taste of the power that magic can offer.

CURE WOUNDS SCHOOL: EVOCATION

With *cure wounds*, a target you touch is healed. Their wounds knit without scars or bruises left behind. More severe injuries may require multiple castings of the spell to heal fully.

SPELL TIPS

- A *cure wounds* spell can heal injuries received in battle, including burns or other traumas, but it cannot halt poison, cure disease, or return life to the dead. More powerful magic is needed for such tasks.

- Although this spell can be cast at first level, it can also be empowered at a higher level in order to mend more grievous injuries. The more power a caster uses, the more damage that can be healed.

DISGUISE SELF

SCHOOL: ILLUSION

Disguise self makes you look like someone else for one hour, fooling people into thinking your appearance has changed. This includes your clothes, armor, and possessions. They're not real physical changes though, so if someone tries to grab an illusionary hat, they'll reach right through and touch your head instead! If you're careful about how you use it, this basic illusion can be very effective.

SPELL TIPS

- Your new appearance must be relatively close to your actual form. You can't make it look like you're a giant or turn from a tall person into a halfling with this spell.

- Stay out of reach, or people quickly realize that your physical form doesn't match what they see!

- This spell affects only your visual appearance. Your voice, scent, and other physical cues will still be your own.

- Intelligent creatures may be able to see through your disguise, so don't assume you'll be able to trick everyone with this.

MAGIC MISSILE SCHOOL: EVOCATION

A *magic missile* spell creates three glowing darts of magical force that you can send hurtling toward a target. These missiles don't cause a lot of damage individually, but if you get zapped by all three they can really hurt. This is a classic combat spell used by many wizards to defend against threats.

SPELL TIPS

- These aren't physical darts, so they effortlessly move through wind, rain, and even armor. All a wizard has to do is point toward their target, and *zap!*

- After about forty yards, these missiles fizzle, so make sure your target is within range before you cast the spell.

- Powerful wizards can create more than three missiles at a time. So if you see a wizard with four or more missiles floating nearby, watch out!

SPEAK WITH ANIMALS

SCHOOL: DIVINATION

The *speak with animals* spell allows you to understand and verbally communicate with beasts for up to ten minutes at a time. Striking up conversations with local wildlife is a good way to find out what's happening in the area.

SPELL TIPS

- Most animals aren't very smart compared to people. Don't expect complex conversations or detailed descriptions.

- Just because you can speak to an animal doesn't mean they'll be your friend. Some animals are angry, hungry, or just want to be left alone!

SECOND LEVEL

Second-level spells are sure to dazzle the untrained; but a skilled spellcaster probably won't be impressed.

BARKSKIN SCHOOL: TRANSMUTATION

Casting this spells gives yourself (or another willing creature) tough, barklike skin that protects you as if you're wearing armor made of wood. This bark protection can last up to an hour, as long as you maintain concentration.

SPELL TIPS

- Barskin doesn't have the weight or bulkiness of metal armor, so it's a good temporary option for rogues, rangers, or other adventurers trying to stay sneaky.

- Having rough barkskin can also help you hide in a forest.

- Since this skin protection is magical, it's not actual wood, so you don't have to worry about termites (any more than you would normally).

INVISIBILITY SCHOOL: ILLUSION

A creature you touch (either yourself or someone else) becomes invisible for up to an hour, as long as you maintain concentration. Anything the target is wearing or carrying is also invisible as long as the *invisibility* spell lasts.

SPELL TIPS

- Attacking a target or casting another spell while invisible will end the effect.

- More powerful spellcasters can turn multiple targets invisible at the same time.

- Invisibility is great for sneaking around, just remember that the spell only hides you from being seen. It doesn't make you silent or muffle your footsteps.

MIRROR IMAGE SCHOOL: ILLUSION

The *mirror image* spell creates three illusionary versions of the caster that mimic their movements, constantly shifting position so observers can't figure out which one is real. Enemies can try to attack these illusions and destroy them, reducing the duplicates until the original is the only one left, but doing so wastes precious time—and in combat, every second counts.

SPELL TIPS

- This spell lasts for exactly one minute, so make sure you cast it only at the most opportune time.

- Attacks that strike a large area may destroy multiple mirror doubles at the same time, dispelling the illusion.

- Creatures whose senses don't rely on sight, like those with extraordinary hearing or an advanced sense of smell, can tell the difference between mirror doubles and reality.

WEB SCHOOL: CONJURATION

Casting a *web* spell creates a mass of sticky webbing in front of you, anchoring on any walls, trees, or other spaces to which it can attach. Creatures who try to move past the webs may be caught in them and get stuck. Very nimble or strong creatures may be able to break free, but most regular humanoids will find themselves caught for up to an hour, or until the caster stops concentrating and lets the *web* spell dissipate.

SPELL TIPS

- Make sure you have surfaces to anchor your *web* spell. Otherwise, the webbing you create will just collapse on itself.

- These magical webs are flammable, so lighting them on fire can be a quick way to get rid of them. Doing so will also burn anything still caught in the strands.

- *Web* spells are normally used against enemies, but a quick-thinking spellcaster can also use them to save people who are falling or to detect invisible creatures.

THIRD LEVEL

More impressive in their effect, these spells also demand more power to cast and more time to master.

FLY SCHOOL: TRANSMUTATION

With the *fly* spell, you, or someone you touch, gains the ability to fly through the air. You can move about as fast as you would normally run, so birds and other naturally flying creatures can easily outrace you, but it's still a lot better than trudging along on the ground.

SPELL TIPS

➤ A *fly* spell lasts for only ten minutes, so make sure you're close to the ground when time is running out.

➤ Powerful magic users can cast this spell on multiple targets at once, allowing an entire group to fly at the same time.

CALL LIGHTNING
SCHOOL: CONJURATION

Casting a *call lightning* spell creates a storm cloud in the sky above. Every few seconds, you can choose a spot and lightning will rain down from the cloud to hit that area. If you maintain concentration, you can launch lightning this way toward different spots, striking enemies or sending them running for cover to try and avoid being blasted.

SPELL TIPS

- This spell only works outside or in areas with a ceiling one hundred feet or higher. Without that much space, there isn't enough atmosphere to conjure a storm cloud.

- If you cast this spell while there's already a storm raging, you'll take control of the existing storm clouds instead and can enhance their power.

- This spell can be quite powerful, but concentrating on controlling the cloud can leave you vulnerable to attack. Make sure you have other adventurers around to help protect you.

SPEAK WITH DEAD

SCHOOL: NECROMANCY

Casting a *speak with dead* spell allows you to converse with the spirit of a deceased creature or person and ask them up to five questions. Finding out how someone died and what to look out for can help you and your fellow heroes from meeting the same fate during a quest.

SPELL TIPS

➤ An apparition summoned with this spell can only speak languages and give information based on what it knew in life. Translation is not included as part of this spell.

➤ This spell doesn't work on undead creatures, since they're not actually dead!

➤ The dead aren't compelled to tell you the truth just because you ask them something. They can lie, tell riddles, or refuse to give information if they don't trust you.

WATER BREATHING

SCHOOL: TRANSMUTATION

This spell gives up to ten creatures (you and/or your allies) the ability to breathe underwater for up to twenty-four hours. Anyone affected by this spell also retains their normal breathing abilities as well, so if you normally breathe air, you can still do that while this spell is active.

SPELL TIPS

➤ Being able to breathe underwater is a powerful ability, but it doesn't automatically mean that you know how to swim or can do it well. If you're planning to adventure underwater, you'll want to get additional training in how to move and fight underwater.

➤ Breathing underwater doesn't let you communicate with fish or other aquatic creatures, but you could combine this with a *speak with animals* spell (see page 41) to travel underwater *and* chat with the locals at the same time.

FOURTH LEVEL

A spellcaster needs real experience under their belt to cast these spells.

FIRE SHIELD SCHOOL: EVOCATION

Once a *fire shield* spell is cast, a barrier of fire appears around your body, lighting up the nearby area and protecting you at the same time. You can choose to activate this spell as a "warm shield" to protect against ice, snow, and cold climates or attacks, or as a "chill shield" to protect against fire and heat.

SPELL TIPS

- This spell can last up to ten minutes, which makes it useful for combat against fire- or ice-based enemies; however, it isn't going to keep you safe for a long time if you're outside in a snowstorm or exploring a volcano.

- You can use the light that this spell emits instead of carrying a torch, freeing up your hands for other things.

ICE STORM
SCHOOL: EVOCATION

Casting an *ice storm* spell summons a torrent of rock-hard ice chunks that rain down from above, pounding the ground in a twenty-foot circular area of your choosing. Targets within the area are hit by these hailstones and their skin begins to freeze.

SPELL TIPS

- An *ice storm* spell not only hurts enemies, it also slows them down as they struggle to move against the wind and keep their footing on the slippery and uneven frozen ground created by its power.

- This spell can put out fires, just as long as you're not worried about damaging anything within the area of effect.

POLYMORPH SCHOOL: TRANSMUTATION

The *polymorph* spell transforms a creature in your field of vision, along with all the gear and weapons they're carrying when the spell activates, into a non-magical beast. If you maintain concentration, this transformation will last up to an hour.

SPELL TIPS

- You can use this spell against enemies to turn them into something harmless or as a way to help friends escape by skittering or flying away.

- If a transformed target is knocked unconscious, they turn back to their original form.

- Transformed people can't speak, cast spells, or perform actions that require complex hand movements or speech, which means that casting *polymorph* on another spellcaster can be a powerful way to stop them from casting spells on you or your friends.

STONE SHAPE SCHOOL: TRANSMUTATION

After casting a *stone shape* spell, you can touch a small stone object or area of stone five feet across or deep and form it into any shape you choose. That means you can make a small passage, mold stone to make a small statue, or even make a small weapon out of rock.

SPELL TIPS

- Get creative! You could pull up a section of stone from the floor to block a door while trying to escape from creatures chasing you, hide an item in a space you carve out in a wall, or drill a small peephole into a barrier to see what's on the other side.

- If you use *stone shape* to make a hole, remember that you'll need to cast the spell again if you want to close it afterward.

FIFTH LEVEL

Mastery of these powerful spells reflects hard work, study, and a deep internal store of magical power.

ANIMATE OBJECTS

After casting an *animate objects* spell, you can choose up to ten small objects (or smaller numbers of larger objects) to come to life and follow your command. Doors will open or slam shut, chains will try to ensnare creatures, and free-floating objects will guard, attack, or defend as you direct them, for up to a minute as long as you maintain concentration.

SPELL TIPS

- Animated objects don't have any personality. They can't speak and won't be able to relay any information.

- If an enemy smashes an object, it reverts to its original form and is no longer animated.

FLAME STRIKE SCHOOL: EVOCATION

The *flame strike* spell summons a vertical column of fire that drops down from above, burning anything within a ten-foot radius of where you direct it. This spell is particularly effective against undead creatures, as it hurts them with both holy light and fire at the same time.

SPELL TIPS

- Area-of-effect spells such as *flame strike* can hurt multiple enemies at the same time if you plan carefully. Look for areas where enemies are gathered close together and use it there for maximum effect.

- Flashy spells such as this one can be quite impressive on the battlefield, but they also call a lot of attention to themselves. That can make you a target for enemies who want to avoid being hit by future spells.

TREE STRIDE SCHOOL: CONJURATION

Casting a *tree stride* spell allows you to step into a tree and then instantly step out from another tree of the same type up to five hundred feet away. You can do this as many times as you want for up to a minute, shifting between trees at will. This power is used by forest creatures and fairy folk to spy on targets or to escape from attackers. Some druids and rangers have learned to do this as well.

SPELL TIPS

- Use this spell to sneak up on an enemy in a forest or to get to the top of an incredibly tall tree faster than you could climb it.

- As soon as you step into a tree with this spell, you sense where all the trees of the same type are within five hundred feet; so you can plan your movement and stay ahead of anyone trying to keep an eye on you.

HOLD MONSTER SCHOOL: ENCHANTMENT

When you cast a *hold monster* spell on a creature, it will magically paralyze them, keeping the beast from moving or attacking for up to a minute, as long as you maintain concentration.

SPELL TIPS

- Using this spell on a powerful foe is a good way to keep it from attacking while your allies defeat smaller and less-dangerous creatures, giving you a strategic advantage.

- Creatures with strong minds may be able to overpower your will and escape, so be careful against highly intelligent monsters.

SIXTH LEVEL

Spellcasters of this level have a well-earned reputation that proceeds them on their travels, and likely a few heroic ballads to celebrate their achievements.

CREATE UNDEAD — SCHOOL: NECROMANCY

The *create undead* spell can only be cast at night; when cast, it turns up to three humanoid corpses into undead creatures called *ghouls*! After being created, ghouls feed on humanoid flesh. They hunt in packs and tend to lurk near places where bodies can be found—graveyards, crypts, and battlefields. These ghouls will follow your commands for twenty-four hours.

SPELL TIPS

- If you want to maintain control of the ghouls for another twenty-four hours, you'll need to re-cast the spell.

- A ghoul's touch can paralyze their target, leaving you helpless for up to a minute. That's more than enough time for a ghoul pack to turn you into their latest feast, so watch out!

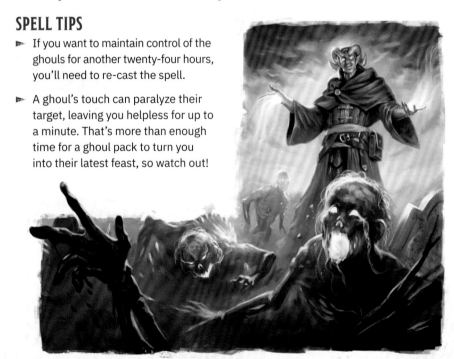

FLESH TO STONE

SCHOOL: TRANSMUTATION

Casting a *flesh to stone* spell at a target attempts to petrify their flesh, turning them into stone. Every few seconds, the creature may try to resist the effect. But if its will is weaker than yours, the target will harden and turn to stone. If you can maintain concentration for a full minute, then the stone transformation is permanent (until it is dispelled through more powerful magic).

SPELL TIPS

► Turning a creature to stone permanently can be quite difficult. But if a creature is even temporarily slowed down by this spell, it can lend a strategic advantage to an adventuring party in combat.

► If a petrified creature is damaged while in stone form, it will have that same damage when returned to its original form.

HEROES' FEAST
SCHOOL: CONJURATION

Casting a *heroes' feast* spell creates a huge banquet of food that up to a dozen creatures can enjoy at the same time. It will take more than an hour to get through this enchanted meal, but at the end of this repast everyone who has eaten will feel healthy and cured of sickness.

SPELL TIPS

➤ Spells such as *heroes' feast* may not seem as powerful as conjuring fire or speaking with the dead, but group morale is very important. A magical meal like this can lift spirits and ready an adventuring party for difficult times ahead.

➤ Magical food has benefits that last beyond the duration of the meal itself. For the next twenty-four hours, anyone who ate feels stronger and braver.

OTTO'S IRRESISTIBLE DANCE
SCHOOL: ENCHANTMENT

When you choose a target and cast *Otto's irresistible dance*, that creature begins a comic dance on the spot, shuffling and tapping its feet for up to a minute, if you maintain concentration. Not only does this look ridiculous, it can also create confusion among enemies as they wonder why their cohort won't stop dancing around when they should be fighting you and your allies!

SPELL TIPS

➤ Like *hold monster* (see page 57), *Otto's irresistible dance* can be a useful way to keep powerful enemies occupied while your allies deal with lesser threats.

➤ A creature that's dancing can still try to attack anyone who gets close to them, but it's much more difficult than normal.

SEVENTH LEVEL

Nearing the peak of magical power available to mortals, these spells are truly impressive.

PRISMATIC SPRAY
SCHOOL: EVOCATION

The *prismatic spray* spell conjures seven multicolored rays of light that flash from your hand, blasting enemies with powerful magic. Each ray is a different color and has a different power.

Red: Fire
Orange: Acid
Yellow: Lightning
Green: Poison
Blue: Ice
Indigo: Paralysis
Violet: Blindness

SPELL TIPS

☞ Not all creatures are vulnerable to the same kinds of magic, so do your research on monsters and creatures so you know which kind of prismatic spray to cast against them.

☞ This spell can't tell friend from foe, so make sure your allies aren't in range when you let it blast.

RESURRECTION SCHOOL: NECROMANCY

There are many lesser healing spells, but the ultimate curative power is to bring a fallen ally back from death itself. As long as a soul is free and willing to return, and they did not die of old age, this spell restores a being to life and cures them of all damage that afflicted them before they passed. Even still, returning from the dead is quite exhausting and it can take several days for a person to return to full strength.

SPELL TIPS

- This powerful spell can resurrect beings who have been deceased for fewer than 100 years; but the longer a target has been dead, the more draining it is on the caster.

- Many spells have components, special ingredients required to fuel their magic. A *resurrection* spell requires a valuable diamond as its component, and casting the spell destroys the diamond instantly. Powerful magic can get quite expensive.

PLANE SHIFT
SCHOOL: CONJURATION

Casting a *plane shift* spell allows you and up to eight other
creatures who link hands to teleport to another dimensional plane.
A physical component is necessary to complete this spell; in this
case, a forked metal rod. There are many dimensions beyond our
own and great treasures to be found in those worlds, but great
danger as well. Such a trip is not to be taken lightly.

SPELL TIPS

- You can specify a destination in general terms with this spell, but not land with pinpoint accuracy.

- This spell can be cast on unwilling targets as well, banishing them from your current dimension.

PLANES OF EXISTENCE

There are a multitude of worlds, as
well as myriad alternate dimensions of
reality, called the planes of existence.
Some are made of pure energy or
raw elemental forces (earth, air, fire,
and water), others are realms of
pure thought or ideology, and others
still may be home to deities or the
demonic. Saving a city or a country
can make an adventurer a hero, but
questing in other worlds and saving
entire dimensions can make a legend.

DIVINE WORD

SCHOOL: EVOCATION

This potent spell calls forth a tiny piece of the power that shaped creation. Any enemies you choose within thirty feet that can hear this sound are struck by its magical force, which may deafen, blind, or stun them. Weaker creatures may even be destroyed completely by its might.

SPELL TIPS

- In addition to damaging regular creatures, *divine word* may cause targets who are from a different plane of existence to be sent back to their home dimension.

- Area-of-effect spells such as *divine word* are an incredibly useful way to stop large groups of smaller creatures from overwhelming an adventuring party.

EIGHTH LEVEL

Few spellcasters reach this level of power, but those who do are nearly unstoppable.

CLONE SCHOOL: NECROMANCY

The curious *clone* spell grows an inert duplicate of a living creature to act as a safeguard against death. Once the process begins, it takes about four months for the clone to be fully grown. After that, if the *original* creature is killed, then their soul will transfer to the duplicate and they will live again. Pretty neat, huh?

SPELL TIPS

- The clone has all the memories, personality, and abilities of the original being from which it was copied, but none of their equipment, so make sure the clone has clothes and weapons once it wakes up.

- A clone can be created to reach maturity at a younger age than the original. Some spellcasters charge a fortune to rich patrons looking to extend their life using this powerful magic spell.

DOMINATE MONSTER SCHOOL: ENCHANTMENT

After casting a *dominate monster* spell on a creature, you attempt to exert your will upon it and take control of its mind and actions. If you succeed and can maintain concentration, then the monster is yours to command for up to an hour. The creature will follow your directions to the best of its ability.

SPELL TIPS

- If a creature is hurt while under this spell, it will be easier for its mind to fight back and break your control over it.

- Creatures without proper minds, including constructs, oozes, and some undead, are immune to charm spells such as this.

EARTHQUAKE SCHOOL: EVOCATION

The powerful *earthquake* spell creates a massive seismic disturbance. Any creatures in its area of effect may be knocked off their feet, thrown into the air, or fall into fissures that open up in the ground beneath them. If this spell is cast in an area where there are buildings or other structures, they are damaged as well and may collapse, causing even more destruction and danger for anyone within range.

SPELL TIPS

- Large-scale destructive spells such as *earthquake* are extremely potent but must be directed with caution, otherwise your allies may end up feeling the effects and be hurt by it as well.

- Casting this spell while inside a building is also extremely dangerous, as the structure may end up collapsing on top of you!

MAZE SCHOOL: CONJURATION

Casting a *maze* spell sends the target creature to a pocket dimension filled with a complex labyrinth. If you can maintain concentration, this labyrinthine banishment will last up to ten minutes, more than enough time to finish off other foes during a battle and prepare for your enemy's return.

SPELL TIPS

- If the target trapped in the maze can find their way to the exit, they'll return to the point from which they vanished.

- Minotaurs can automatically solve these magical mazes, so don't waste this powerful spell on them.

NINTH LEVEL

The most potent spells imaginable, these awesome powers defy the laws of the universe.

METEOR SWARM
SCHOOL: EVOCATION

The mighty *meteor swarm* spell summons blazing orbs of burning stone that plummet to the ground with unmatched force, destroying almost anything unfortunate enough to be in their way. Every creature in a forty-foot radius is pummeled and burned by the heat of these meteors, and anything combustible an individual is wearing may burst into flame.

SPELL TIPS

- *Meteor swarm* is one of those "go for broke" spells that can cause massive destruction, but also change the course of a desperate battle.

- A poorly aimed spell with this kind of power can easily wipe out allies or ravage buildings and terrain, so choose your targets carefully.

TIME STOP
SCHOOL: TRANSMUTATION

When the impressive *time stop* spell is cast, the flow of time is halted for everyone but the caster. For up to thirty seconds, you can move and use your equipment without anyone within one thousand feet even knowing that it's happening. When time resumes, those within that space will believe whatever changed did so instantaneously.

This spell ends if you interact with anything you're not personally carrying, including other creatures, or if you move beyond one thousand feet from where the spell was cast.

SPELL TIPS

- A *time stop* spell is the perfect way to make your escape when things have gone wrong. It's also a useful way to change your position in a battle or drink a much-needed healing potion.

- Unfortunately you can't stop the flow of time for anyone else, so using this spell with your allies is impossible.

SHAPECHANGE
SCHOOL: TRANSMUTATION

Casting a *shapechange* spell causes you to transform into a beast or magical creature. You can keep changing form into different creatures for up to an hour, as long as you maintain your concentration throughout. You will take on any of the physical attributes of the creature you have become, but keep your own mind and personality throughout any and all transformations. With this spell, you could temporarily become a dragon, a unicorn, a beholder, or any other creature you've encountered on your travels.

SPELL TIPS

➤ When the spell activates, decide if your clothing and equipment falls away, merges into your body, or is worn (only if it fits). Clothes and equipment won't change size or shape.

➤ You can only speak if your chosen form also has the ability to speak.

WEIRD
SCHOOL: ILLUSION

A *weird* spell creates a potent illusion that reaches into the minds of your enemies and creates a vision of nightmare creatures formed from their deepest fears. These imaginary monsters attack inside your opponents' minds, but your adversaries can't tell what's real and what isn't as they struggle to escape. All your targets within a three-hundred-foot radius will be hurt by these mental terrors until they either muster the willpower to resist or are destroyed.

SPELL TIPS

➤ Since this is a psychic attack happening within your target's imagination, you can't see what it is they're fighting.

➤ Although targets of this spell are not being physically attacked, if they die in their mind they will also die in the real world.

WILD MAGIC

Wild magic is born from the uncontrolled forces of chaos beneath the order of creation. In some cases, it comes from being exposed to a surge of raw magic from an ancient, arcane source. In others, the sorcerer may have been blessed by a fairy or marked by a demon. Still other instances seem to be as chaotic as wild magic itself, power surging through the sorcerer's body for no apparent reason. Only sorcerers are able to access this magical power, which defies all attempts to study and codify it.

As the name suggests, wild magic is often tricky to control. A sorcerer fueled by wild magic is capable of astonishing feats, but using this power can have unpredictable side effects. These effects are known as a *wild magic surge*. There's no way to know when a surge will strike, or what form it will take, although they often occur at the most awkward (or funny) moments.

BEND LUCK

One pleasant aspect of wild magic is the ability, as a sorcerer grows in power, to use that chaos to swing the fates in your favor. Experienced sorcerers can learn to "bend luck," which increases the chances that their spells will have the desired effect on their target. Of course, using this ability carries a risk of a wild magic surge, making things even more unpredictable.

WILD MAGIC SURGE

Here are some examples of wild magic surges; but since the effects are random, you can always invent your own to add to the list!

- You grow a long beard of feathers, which lasts until you sneeze. Then they all fly off your face at once!

- Three creatures within thirty feet of you are struck by a bolt of lightning out of the blue.

- You are transformed into a sheep for ten minutes.

- For one minute, you cannot speak. Pink bubbles float out of your mouth when you try.

- When you speak, it's incredibly loud, no matter what, for one minute.

- Your skin turns a vibrant shade of blue, which lasts until the curse is removed through other powerful magic.

- You are teleported sixty feet in a random direction.

- A unicorn appears within five feet of you, but disappears after five minutes.

- You accidentally cast a *fireball* spell on yourself.

- Your hair all falls out! It will regrow to its original length over the next twenty-four hours.

- You can't be hurt for one minute.

- Illusory flower petals and butterflies appear in the air around your head for ten minutes.

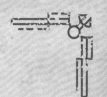

MAGICAL ITEMS

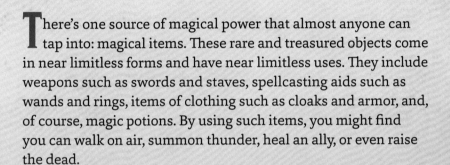

There's one source of magical power that almost anyone can tap into: magical items. These rare and treasured objects come in near limitless forms and have near limitless uses. They include weapons such as swords and staves, spellcasting aids such as wands and rings, items of clothing such as cloaks and armor, and, of course, magic potions. By using such items, you might find you can walk on air, summon thunder, heal an ally, or even raise the dead.

Magical items are not easy to come by. You may uncover a powerful gemstone hidden deep in a dangerous dungeon, seize a magical sword from a vanquished foe, or receive a useful potion as a reward for a good deed. Gaining magic items requires a combination of courage and luck. Some magical items are common enough that you could buy them from a shopkeeper or a traveling salesperson on a lucky day; but beware, there are many counterfeits out there!

ATTUNEMENT

Most magical items require attunement, a special bond created when you spend an hour or more holding the item and focusing on its use. That may mean meditating on a magic ring, practicing with an enchanted sword, or studying a book.

You can only attune a maximum of three magical items at one time. The magical items on the following pages require attunement unless stated otherwise.

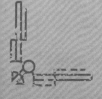

WEAPONS

Weapons are common and popular types of magical items, because even when the magic part doesn't come in handy, the weapon part just might.

Magic swords are especially celebrated. Many great heroes of legend carried famous swords that could sing, light themselves on fire, or never miss a stroke. However, there are magical versions of every type of weapon you might imagine, from bows and arrows to war hammers or hand axes.

DAGGER OF VENOM By focusing on the Dagger of Venom, you can make it exude a thick black poison that coats the blade for up to a minute. Anyone cut by the dagger may succumb to its poison. It does not require attunement.

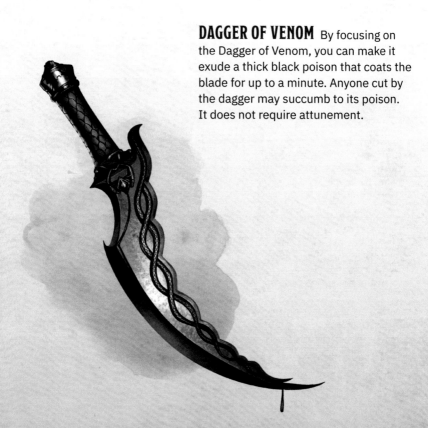

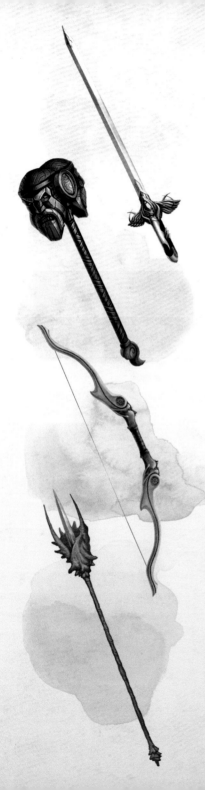

DANCING SWORD

When hurled into the air, the Dancing Sword can be directed to strike like a missile at whatever nearby enemy you choose. If luck is on your side, it might attack up to four different foes before flying back to your hand.

HAMMER OF THUNDERBOLTS

The Hammer of Thunderbolts gives you such great strength that you might survive going toe-to-toe with a giant! You can also use it to hurl thunderbolts at your enemies. However, the hammer's powers can only be accessed by someone wearing magical armor that gives them a giant's strength.

OATHBOW

The Oathbow is an elvish weapon that invites its owner to identify a "sworn enemy." Any arrow you fire will seek out that enemy, no matter the distance. However, the bow expects loyalty and, as long as your sworn enemy lives, you will find it difficult to use any other weapons.

WEAPON OF WARNING

A weapon of warning can take many forms, but all types magically alert you to nearby danger. The weapon will even stir you from sleep when an enemy approaches, saving you from sneak attacks and deadly ambushes.

THE SUNSWORD

The Sunsword was once a particularly fine longsword with a blade made of magically resilient crystal, created by nobleman Sergei von Zarovich. Sergei was murdered by his envious brother, Strahd, who attempted to have the sword destroyed, but the hilt survived.

Imbued with magical will and possessed of a desire to seek vengeance on Strahd, the sword hilt generated its own blade of pure sunlight—the perfect weapon for destroying Strahd, whose hate and dark magics transformed him into a vampire lord. The sunlight blade also makes this sword a great weapon to use against any other undead you encounter!

The Sunsword is a swift weapon that cuts and blasts undead enemies with its radiant light. It can also act as a source of light in the dark. The sword possesses its own mind and can convey emotions to its wielder. For example, it might transmit a sense of fear if it senses danger nearby.

SUN BLADES

The true Sunsword is believed to be lost somewhere deep in the dark recesses of Castle Ravenloft, but other swords with a sunlight blade are known to exist. These swords are known as sun blades. By channeling daylight through their blade, they are capable of delivering deadly strikes against vampires and other undead monstrosities.

STAFFS

A magical staff is generally five to six feet long, about as tall as a regular human, and can be made from a wide range of materials, including wood, metal, or even crystal. They can be polished smooth or twisted and gnarled. Some staffs can be used as a melee weapon in combat, doubling as a quarterstaff. Even a non-spellcaster can use these artifacts to channel mystical power. Each staff has ten charges, which is the number of times it can be used before running out of power, and regains one charge per day, usually at dawn.

Staff of the Adder

Staff of Charming

STAFF OF THE ADDER When you speak a command word, the head of the Staff of the Adder comes to life, transforming into a poisonous snake that you can use to attack opponents. The effect lasts for one minute, so be quick.

STAFF OF CHARMING With the Staff of Charming, you can cast a spell that will charm another person, making them friendly toward you and willing to obey your commands. It also allows you to understand any spoken language.

STAFF OF FROST The wintery Staff of Frost grants you extra resistance to damage from cold and ice. You can also use it to cast a magical spell that will do freezing damage to your enemies.

STAFF OF WITHERING When you use the Staff of Withering to hit a foe, you can choose to inflict special withering damage that's harder to heal, along with the normal physical impact of your melee strike.

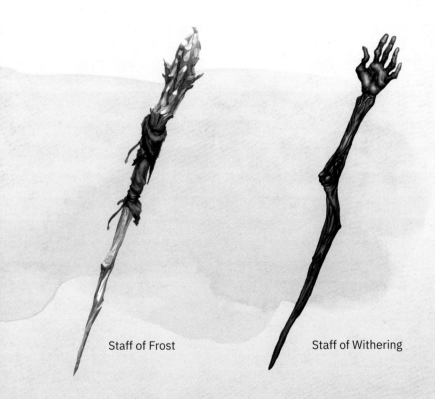

Staff of Frost

Staff of Withering

LEGENDARY STAFF

STAFF OF THE MAGI

The Staff of the Magi is a rare weapon that can be used as a standard quarterstaff in combat; however, its real value lies in its ability to cast and absorb magical attacks. When holding the staff, its possessor can use it to try and absorb any spell cast against them. If successful, the spell's energy is stored within the staff for future use, and the wielder is completely protected from the spell's effects.

The Staff of the Magi is capable of casting up to fifty spells, regaining one spell charge each dawn, along with any charges from spells that it absorbs. Magical attacks include casting fireballs, lightning bolts, ice storms, webs, and even a wall of fire. Its wielder can also use the staff to conjure an elemental servant, pass through solid walls, lift objects with psychic energy, detect magic, or cast an invisible shield to protect against evil.

In a desperate moment, the Staff of the Magi may be used for a single, explosive attack. By breaking the staff, all the magic stored within it is released at once. This retributive strike fills a thirty-foot sphere with explosive energy, wreaking untold amounts of damage and destruction. There is a chance that this explosion will cast the one breaking the staff into an alternate dimension.

WANDS

A magical wand is about fifteen inches long. They can be made from metal, bone, or wood and can be tipped with a charged piece of metal, crystal, stone, or some other material. Similar to staffs, each wand has seven charges that renew each day. If you run out of charges, the wand may be destroyed, so try not to drain it completely!

WAND OF LIGHTNING BOLTS

A twisted metal wand, the Wand of Lightning Bolts allows you to cast a lightning bolt (up to one hundred feet long and five feet wide) in any direction you choose. Be careful, though, because the lightning will set fire to anything flammable in its path!

WAND OF MAGIC DETECTION
Each use of the Wand of Magic Detection allows you to locate any magic power within thirty feet, causing enchanted items or locations to glow with a faint aura. The power lasts for up to ten minutes but this powerful wand has only three charges, so use it wisely.

WAND OF PARALYSIS
The Wand of Paralysis shoots a thin, blue ray that can hit a single target within a sixty-foot radius and paralyze them for up to one minute.

WAND OF POLYMORPH
The creepy-looking Wand of Polymorph can transform its target from one type of creature into a different, less-dangerous type. The target is limited by the restrictions of its new form. For example, a human turned into a sheep would no longer be able to talk or walk upright. The effect lasts for up to one hour.

WAND OF WONDER

One of the most powerful wands in all of existence, the Wand of Wonder can cast a staggering variety of magical spells. The effect is random and targets any one creature of the wielder's choice. Magical effects created by the wand can include:

Butterfly Swarm—a cloud of three hundred oversize butterflies forms around the target. The swarm makes it difficult for the victim to see or move through the space and lasts for ten minutes.

Darkness—a magical darkness surrounds the target in a fifteen-foot sphere. Not even darkvision or non-magical light sources can illuminate this gloom.

Gust of Wind—a strong wind pours out of the wand tip. All creatures in its path are pushed away, while torches and other flames are extinguished.

Heavy Rain—a sudden rainstorm falls around the target, obscuring vision and making everyone very, very wet.

Invisibility—instead of striking a target, this effect works on the wielder, making them invisible to all creatures for up to one minute. The effect vanishes if the wielder attacks anyone.

Slowness—causes the target to move at half their normal speed.

Stinking Cloud—a large sphere of yellow, noxious gas appears around the target, stinking of rotten eggs and skunk.

Thought Detection—the wielder can read the thoughts of their target for up to one minute.

USER BEWARE

Once in a while, the Wand of Wonder will not cast any outward spell. Instead, it simply stuns the wielder for ten seconds, leaving them convinced that something amazing has happened—even though it did nothing at all.

MAGIC ARMOR

Armor can be an adventurer's best friend, keeping you safe from a killing blow when faced with rampaging orcs, elvish arrows, or the slashing claws of a feral creature. Magic armor, though, is an upgrade; it doesn't just protect you from normal attacks, it can deflect magical blows and some have other special abilities you can call upon in the heat of battle.

If you need to wear armor anyway, you might as well try to get some made of magical dragonhide, right? And magic armor doesn't just include mail and chest plates. It can also include shields, bracers, or helmets.

ANIMATED SHIELD

An animated shield can float in the air in front of its wielder for up to a minute, protecting them from attacks. That makes it a great form of defense if you want to wield a weapon in each hand while staying protected.

BRACERS OF ARCHERY
Mastering a new weapon can take years of practice, and time is short. Thankfully there are types of magic armor that can take the hassle of training out of the equation. These bracers, fashioned from enchanted arrows, turn their attuned wearer into a master archer for as long as they're worn.

DWARVEN PLATE
Sometimes the best magical armor is also the toughest, and dwarves make *really* tough armor! A suit of dwarven plate mail magically protects you from damage and enhances your ability in combat, making you a more effective warrior on the field of battle.

HELM OF TELEPORTATION
Sometimes you find yourself so deep in trouble that your only real chance is a quick getaway, and that's when a helm of teleportation comes in handy. It can transport you and your nearby allies to a new location in the blink of an eye.

POTIONS

Potions are magical liquids made from enchanted herbs and other arcane ingredients, by experienced spellcasters who have spent years, if not decades, perfecting the art of capturing magic in a bottle.

A potion is a one-time-use magical item. You must drink the whole thing to get the special effect, so they can't be shared among multiple party members (unless you have multiple potions!). Once ingested, a potion takes effect right away, so be sure to save them for just the right moment.

POTION OF FLYING Drinking a potion of flying will allow you to fly for up to one hour. However, you can move only as fast as your character can walk on land. You can also hover in place. Be aware that you will start to fall the instant the potion wears off, so keep track of the time from ingestion.

POTION OF CLAIRVOYANCE
A potion of clairvoyance allows you to either see or hear what is happening in the moment at any location you have visited or seen before. You can also use it to see around corners or behind obstacles that are near your current location. The effect lasts for up to ten minutes, and you can switch between sight and hearing by focusing for six seconds.

POTION OF HEALING
An adventurer's best friend, a potion of healing will restore your body from damage sustained during a fight. Regular potions of healing repair minor wounds and bruises, while rarer types can do even more. Indeed, a potion of supreme healing will mend broken bones and fix deadly injuries in an instant.

POTION OF WATER BREATHING
The cloudy green potion of water breathing allows you to breathe underwater for sixty minutes. It smells—and tastes—as salty as the sea. Like the potion of flying, it wears off immediately once the hour is over, so don't let yourself get into deep waters without a plan of escape for when your time is up.

POISON POTION

Not all potions are friendly! Some nasty concoctions may look like a potion of healing but have effects that are the exact opposite. The unwary adventurer who imbibes this liquid will find themselves losing health fast. Only an *identify* spell, which can be learned by bards and wizards, is able to dispel the illusion that makes the poison potion look so sweet.

RINGS

Magical rings are a popular type of enchanted item, because they are small and discreet. As a result, your enemies don't always know you have them, or that you're about to use them, and you never need to be parted from them. (Nice jewelry can also really complete an outfit.)

A magic ring is like having a bonus spell at your fingertips—though it's really closer to your knuckle! Just remember that you can be attuned to only three magical items at once, so wearing a bunch of different rings doesn't necessarily mean you'll be able to access all their powers simultaneously.

RING OF THE RAM The Ring of the Ram generates a spectral battering ram that can smash through obstacles—including other people. Up to three times a day, you can use this ring like a long-distance super-punch to shatter doors or knock people off their feet.

RING OF ANIMAL INFLUENCE
If you want to charm an animal to be your friend, frighten an animal to chase it away, or communicate with an animal so that you understand each other, wearing this ring will empower you to do any or all of these things. This ring does not require attunement.

RING OF REGENERATION
An incredibly useful item for anyone who likes to dive into the thick of danger. The Ring of Regeneration allows its wearer to heal quickly from injury. Even if someone chops off part of your body, this ring will allow you to grow it back! (One important note: This kind of magical regeneration doesn't work if the part that's chopped off is your head.)

RING OF SHOOTING STARS
This ring has several powerful effects. For example, it can generate dazzling light, or create balls of lightning that can shock anyone who comes near. However, its most useful effect is that it allows its wearer to fire shooting stars from their hands, which can burn anyone they strike! This ring can only be attuned at night.

CLOAKS

More than just clothing items to keep you warm and dry, magical cloaks can bestow wondrous powers upon their wearer. They can be worn by all character classes with no magical training required. Like all wearable magic items, cloaks are designed to be adjustable for all sizes, from tiny gnomes to towering dragonborn. Some cloaks even have, woven right into their fabric, the magical ability to change their size.

CLOAK OF DISPLACEMENT

The Cloak of Displacement casts an illusion that makes you appear to be standing just a little bit away from your actual location, making it much harder for enemies to hit you. If you *are* hit, the cloak's power stops working for a few seconds. If you are restrained, unconscious, or otherwise unable to move, the displacement illusion also stops functioning.

CLOAK OF ARACHNIDA

The spider-patterned Cloak of Arachnida allows you to climb as easily as you can walk, moving across vertical surfaces and upside down along ceilings. It also makes you resistant to poison and prevents you from being caught in webs. Once per day, you can create a sticky web up to twenty feet wide that can ensnare creatures.

CLOAK OF ELVENKIND

The Cloak of Elvenkind is an elvish garment that lets the wearer, when the cloak's hood is placed over their head, draw upon the natural stealth and perception of the elven race. The cloak's power makes it harder for you to be seen when worn this way, while enhancing your ability to hide by shifting colors to provide camouflage.

CLOAK OF THE MANTA RAY

Worn with the hood up, the Cloak of the Manta Ray grants you the ability to breathe underwater and swim as fast as a medium-size fish. The effects stop when the hood is lowered.

WONDROUS ITEMS

Wondrous magic items are ones that don't fall into any of the previous categories. They can range from wearable items, like boots and gloves, to uncommon jewelry such as circlets and broaches. Bags, ropes, carpets, crystal balls, musical instruments, and other uncommon objects also fall into this classification. This magical designation is limited only by your imagination!

MASK OF THE BEAST

These ornately beautiful masks contain a spell that can render an animal docile and friendly; most useful when the wearer wants to survive an encounter with a predator such as a big cat or a beast such as a charging bull. It's equally effective on less-threatening creatures, from fish to birds or even monkeys.

The wearer cannot directly command animals nor speak their language, but finds it easy to interact in ways not otherwise possible. For example, they might convince a lion to let them ride on its back, or ask a bear to attack an intruder. More powerful druids and sorcerers can target multiple creatures, and run with a pack of wolves or swim among sharks without any fear.

BAG OF HOLDING

This bag appears to be relatively small, about two feet tall and four feet long, but it can hold up to sixty-four cubic feet worth of stuff. (That's about the size of four regular refrigerators.) Objects placed in the bag can weigh up to 500 pounds, but the bag itself will never weigh more than 15 pounds, similar to the weight of an average house cat. Overloading the bag causes its contents to vanish to another dimension, so keep track of how much you've stuffed inside.

BOOTS OF SPEED

Click together the heels of a pair of boots of speed and your walking velocity will instantly double. On top of that, your reaction to attacks is increased, making it harder for enemies to get the jump on you. The magic wears off after ten minutes, and will not recover until you've had a long, eight-hour rest. You can turn the boots' magic off by clicking your heels together a second time, saving part of the magical charge for later use.

LANTERN OF REVEALING

When lit, this lantern gives off a bright light that renders invisible creatures and objects visible. This light extends in a thirty-foot circle around the lantern. By lowering the lantern's hood, you can focus the light's range to five feet.

NOLZUR'S MARVELOUS PIGMENTS These very rare pigments allow you to create three-dimensional objects by painting them onto a flat surface. Each pot of paint can cover up to one thousand square feet, about the floor size of a small suburban house. When you complete the painting, the object or landscape becomes a real, physical object. Painting a door on a wall creates a real door you can walk through, for example. It is not possible to paint wealth or magic into being. Painted gold coins will turn out to be dull, worthless metal, and painted wands cannot be used for spells.

ORB OF DRAGONKIND The rare and wondrous orbs of dragonkind allow their user to *summon* a dragon. They don't grant any other control over the powerful beasts; all you're really doing is bringing one of the most formidable creatures in the world much *closer* to you. What they do when they arrive is up to them. Often, they'll want to punish the summoner! An orb grants other powers at random, such as healing or immunities; however, it also curses its wielder with unexpected weaknesses and disadvantages. Using an orb is very risky.

ROPE OF CLIMBING

By holding one end of this magical rope and speaking a command word, the rope animates, moving toward the destination of your choosing. You can tell the rope to fasten itself (securing to an object), untie itself, or knot itself in one-foot intervals for easier climbing. The rope is sixty feet long and can hold up to 3,000 pounds in weight.

STACKING MAGICAL ITEMS

Except in rare instances, a character can wear or use only one of each type of magical item at a time. Stacking multiple magic cloaks over your clothing, for instance, is not only very warm and bulky but can negate the effect of the magic.

For paired magical items, like boots or gloves, you must wear both the right and left items for the magic to work—so no sharing your boots of speed with a friend so you can both run double-time.

USING MAGIC
TO TELL YOUR OWN STORIES

Bel Vala could hear footsteps on the cold stone floor and smell touches of exotic fragrances used to mask the stench of death, but there was no breathing to match the animalistic movement she detected.

Undead.

The unliving were her most hated enemies and she would do anything to destroy their evil blight.

The cleric's hands clenched tightly. She could feel the familiar touch of Giver, her enchanted dagger, and Taker, the silver chalice. These linked items would not seem like much to a casual observer, but those who could see magic would be awestruck by their potent aura.

The vampire spawn began to move closer; one breaking the silence of the room with a hissing threat, her tongue pressed against sharp fangs.

"Lord Strahd has marked you for death."

Bel Vala smirked and her hands quivered for a moment as she felt the divine power of her god, Corellon, surging from within.

Pure sunlight exploded from Bel Vala's frail body and the vampires screamed in agony.

Reading about adventure is a great way to stir your imagination, and creating a character is an important first step in composing your personal stories. Building a new character is about discovering who they are at the beginning of their journey and then figuring out who they might become as their legend grows across the land.

Your idea might start with a single hero or a small group of adventurers, but it can go *anywhere*: a creature's lair, the village nearby, cities and dungeons, caverns or skyscapes. You get to choose all the ingredients and stir them together. To help you as you develop your story, here are some questions to keep in mind:

WHO ARE YOUR CHARACTERS?

- Are your heroes like you or different? Young or old, human or something else? Think about the foes you must face. Great heroes require great challenges. What makes your villains memorable and powerful, and what brings them into conflict with your adventurers?

WHERE DOES YOUR STORY TAKE PLACE?

- At the top of a mountain, in a serene forest, deep underwater, or in a creepy boneyard?

WHEN DOES THE STORY HAPPEN?

- At night or during the day, in the middle of a thunderstorm or right before the bells toll to ring in the new year? Think about time passing as your story unfolds.

HOW DO THINGS CHANGE AS THE STORY PROCEEDS?

- Do your heroes succeed or fail? Do they find somewhere new or explore someplace old?

WHAT SHOULD SOMEONE FEEL AS THEY EXPERIENCE YOUR STORY?

- Do you want them to laugh or get scared? Cheer or be grossed out?

WHY ARE YOUR HEROES GOING ON THIS ADVENTURE?

- Knowing what their goals are will help you create a compelling tale of courage and exploration.

Remember, you don't have to answer all these questions by yourself! DUNGEONS & DRAGONS is a collaborative game where you work with your friends to create your own stories. One person acts as a narrator, called a Dungeon Master, and the other players each take on the role of a hero, called a Player Character, in the adventuring party in a story. The Dungeon Master sets up a scene by describing a place and any threats that may exist, and then each player contributes ideas by explaining their own character's actions. With each scene created by the group, the story moves forward in unexpected and entertaining ways.

If you don't feel confident starting from scratch, you can go to your local gaming store and play a DUNGEONS & DRAGONS demonstration session. Demos can be a quick way to learn how the game is played and an opportunity to possibly make some brand-new friends at the same time.

After you've read through all the character options in this little magic manual, there's even more DUNGEONS & DRAGONS material out there to ignite your imagination. The *Monsters & Creatures* guide is bursting at the seams with beasts aplenty for you and your friends to defeat. *Warriors & Weapons* goes into more detail about the different adventuring races and the martial classes who can join you on your quest. The *Dungeons & Tombs* guide is filled with strange, sinister places for you and your friends to explore. You know who your hero is and have imbued them with magical might, now find out what dangers lurk in the darkness and *answer the call to adventure!*

Published in the United States by Ten Speed Press, an imprint of Random House, a division of Penguin Random House LLC, New York.
www.crownpublishing.com
www.tenspeed.com

Ten Speed Press and the Ten Speed Press colophon are registered trademarks of Penguin Random House LLC.

Originally published in the United States in hardcover by Ten Speed Press, an imprint of Random House, a division of Penguin Random House LLC, New York, in 2020.

Publisher: Aaron Wehner
Art Director and Designer: Betsy Stromberg
Editors: Patrick Barb and Julie Bennett
Managing Editor: Doug Ogan
Production Designer: Lisa Bieser
Wizards of the Coast Team: David Gershman, Kate Irwin, Adam Lee, Hilary Ross, Liz Schuh
Illustrations: Conceptopolis, LLC

10 9 8 7

2020 Trade Paperback Boxed Set Edition